MW01681445

For Marv Ragow -

Positively,

Art [signature]

A Dynamic Guide to
Greater Success & Happiness

SELLING LUCKY

By

Art Fettig

ILLUSTRATIONS BY: XENIA ROSE

Fell's Books Fill Your Needs

FREDERICK FELL PUBLISHERS, INC.

New York

To Mom.

To my loving wife Ruth.

To daughters Nancy and Amy.

To my sisters, Virginia, Florence and Barbara.

To the most dynamic women I know, Dottie, Thelma, Merlyn and Eden.

And to all of the women of the world. Though I may not understand them, I love them and stand in awe, at the greatness that is in them.

ISBN: 0-8119-0306-0

For information address:

Frederick Fell Publishers, Inc.
386 Park Avenue South
New York, New York 10016

Published simultaneously in Canada by:
Thomas Nelson & Sons, Limited
Don Mills, Ontario, Canada

MANUFACTURED IN THE UNITED STATES OF AMERICA

1 2 3 4 5 6 7 8 9 0

TABLE OF CONTENTS

PREFACE......

"Selling Lucky" is a book for people who are in the business of selling themselves. That includes everyone. For each of us becomes better at what we are doing once we learn how to work more effectively with others.

Arthur (Red) Motley, Chairman of the Board of Parade Publications became a legend in the sales field for his statement, "Nothing happens until somebody sells something." And yet that statement applies not only to the sales field.

All communication is a form of selling. Teaching demands daily selling. The whole process of dating and courting is a giant sales campaign. A parent child relationship requires selling and persuasion continually. Effective leadership and management demands effective selling every day.

Nothing happens until somebody sells something. And if a whole lot isn't happening in your life then perhaps it is time that you brushed up on your personal selling style.

Selling Lucky is a book for sales people. The ideas and techniques found in this book are concepts that I picked up from many of the most successful people I know. You cannot help but discover useful nuts and bolts know-how that will result in more success for you as you apply these Lucky Ideas to your daily work.

This is the type of book that takes rereading. Most of those who have reviewed it tell me that they devoured it at one sitting. And nearly all begged for the chance to read it again. Many have written how they put a particular idea to work that very day and how amazed they were when they saw the idea working for them exactly as the idea was presented.

One editor wrote that a single idea had immediately improved her total communication technique 100%.

If you will accept the fact that a great deal of what you do every day, no matter what your occupation, involves the technique of selling, then this book may have a profound effect on your future and the success that will come your way.

Selling Lucky probably won't change your results at the card table but it just might really turn you into a winner in Life.

CHAPTER 1

BASICS

This is an idea book. It is filled with lucky ideas. Ideas that have made many of my friends the luckiest people in the world. Some of them are in the sales field but some are in teaching or management or even professional speaking. They all realize that to be successful they first had to learn how to sell themselves to other people. Lucky ideas without action are useless. I hope that this book will help you to become luckier.

"You're lucky, man. . .you are lucky." "Everything you touch seems to turn into money." "You look ten years younger than your age." "Nice home. . .cars, and I understand that you don't have a single mortgage payment." "Lucky, that's the only answer. . .you are luckier than anyone I know."

Whenever I go out and do the things I love to do and come home with a pocket full of reward I know that it is true. I'm Mr. Lucky. I'm lucky to be in the right place at the right time with the right message that audiences will buy. I'm lucky that when I put my camera to my eye I see beautiful things that people will buy. When I put my fingers on the keys of my typewriter I'm lucky because they type out messages that editors will buy.

Bill Gove, a fantastic speaker in the field of sales makes the statement, "People love to buy and I give them every opportunity."

I'm Lucky. . . .and I have always had a lot of luck. When I was losing it was bad luck. Now that I'm winning it is good luck. Winners win and losers lose. Profound, huh? But that is true. You can be a winner or a loser. Lucky or unlucky. The choice is yours.

Now as I looked around at those lucky people I know I learned that nearly all of them are Idea People. They thrive on ideas. They are vitally interested in people behavior and in the way their own minds work. In time they learn about programming their subconscious minds for success. They discover that their brain is a computor and it works on the data we feed it. Feed it creative positive thoughts and you will have a winning life. Feed it negative thoughts and look out.

Let's begin with just two ideas. The two ideas that changed my luck from bad to good. You could probably change your whole future by following these two, but just to make sure, we give you a lot more.

#1 BELIEVE. Write it down. Beat it into your subconscious mind. Believe. Believe in yourself, in your product or service, in your abilities. Believe. Read that belief several times a day. Reinforce it. Act as if your goals were already realities and WHAM! You'll be amazed at how fast your luck develops.

#2 BE ENTHUSIASTIC. That's the key to selling. Selling yourself first. Selling yourself on yourself, and once you've accomplished that you'll find yourself selling yourself to others. ENTHUSIASM. Sure, you know the meaning of the word. . . . "*God like. . .Divinely Inspired.*"

Lucky ideas. Those two alone can make you luckier than you dreamed possible but we want to add to your list of lucky ideas. Here are some more that I discovered. Discovered. . . .not created. . . .not invented. . . .nor did I carry these down from the mountains in Tibet. The word is "discovered."

As with most great ideas, these ideas have been around for a long time. You'll find these same ideas rediscovered again and again by others in years to come.

My good friend Cavett Robert, the busiest speaker and most loved man I ever met, once explained to me. . ."Art, when you take one great idea from every man you meet, that my friend, is research. When you take them all from one person that is grand larceny."

When I look back on all of the exciting ideas that have come my way I visualize the wonderful people who have passed these ideas on to me. I believe the first exposure that I had to a positive new way of life was from a record by Earl Nightengale. The title was "The Strangest Secret" and it started me searching for more answers. Next I read "Think and Grow Rich" by Napoleon Hill. After that I discovered a magazine called Success Unlimited and I read a lot of the positive philosophy of its publisher W. Clement Stone.

Never will I forget the day I received the copy of Success Unlimited that carried an article I had written and the article was back to back with an article by Maxwell Maltz, the author of the great book Psycho Cybernetics.

Ideas. Lucky Ideas. Selling Ideas.

I just hope that my presentation of these ideas will find a home in the chambers of your subconscious mind where you will be able to call upon them daily for greater luck in your life.

In my book, luck is what other people say you have when you begin to receive the rewards you have earned through hard work and creativity and persistence. I hope that these ideas will spark in you lucky ideas of your own so that you soon know the joy of creating your own AHA'S AND AHO'S. New ideas flashing through your mind. New applications of your service or product.

If you are in the sales field I honestly feel that you are already in the luckiest profession you could find.

Now lets get on with more lucky ideas to help you climb into that magic lucky selling circle. The group that is filled with the top 10% in their profession. Those who have discovered the secret of lucky selling.

CHAPTER 2

"GET ON WITH IT!"

"Get on with it!" Those four words. . ."Get on with it!" have done more to add direction to a greater number of people's lives than any four words I can think of. And if there were any ground rules I could set for making this book work for you, they would be the words of Rich DeVos, President of the Amway Corporation: "Get on with it."

Without action, ideas are useless. That is why I would like to suggest that you try to find an immediate application to every idea that you find in this book. Don't sit back and feel comfortable when you can honestly say, "I've heard that idea before." Ideas are like rye grass. You have to reseed every season for the best results.

Now let's talk for a few minutes about Richard M. DeVos, the President of Amway Corporation. He has been "getting on" with it for some time and, because of his outstanding record of get up and go, he has inspired hundreds of thousands of others to take a more positive attitude towards themselves and their futures.

Rich DeVos started his business career when he first came out of the service after World War II. He teamed up with his high school buddy, Jay Van Andel, and they went into the aviation business. Neither of them knew how to fly. When you are young and excited about a business, there often isn't time to learn some things. This proved to be a real advantage to them because, while most people with flying schools were up flying with students, Jay and Rich were out selling more and more students on the idea of flying. Within a short time, they had a number of experienced pilots working for them.

One minor incident during their flying school experience illustrates their "get on with it" philosophy. When they first opened up, they discovered that the local airport runway was not yet completed. They solved this minor problem by installing pontoon floats on their aircraft and taking off and landing on the water.

Of all of the successful people I have met in my life time, the one characteristic I have found in most of them is their ability to overcome minor set-backs creatively. Most losers tell you. . . "I can't do that right now because. . ." The winners say, "I'll get around that obstacle this way."

I once heard Rich DeVos tell an audience that he believed that everyone should go into the restaurant business at least once in their lifetime. "Do it and get it out of your system and then get on with something you can succeed with," he said.

Rich DeVos and Jay Van Andel went into the drive-in restaurant business in Grand Rapids, Michigan. On opening night, when they discovered that the electric company had not yet installed their service, they did what every good quarterback does in such a situation. . .they punted. They rented a generator and "got on with it."

In 1959, the two men started a company that would somehow touch the lives of nearly every American. They began the business in their basements, and maybe it was symbolic. They were building from the ground up. And as with every building job, the foundation often determines the soundness of the structure that is built upon it. If you study the structure of the Amway Corporation, you will find, like I did, that it is sound.

This is not meant to be a commercial, but a corporation usually reflects the philosophy of its founders, and when I study the positive attitudes that made Amway Corporation grow to its present size and its present status of success, I am reminded that the basic attitude of "Get on with It!" is what made America great.

Now. . .about this book and about "Selling Lucky." The ideas that we share in this book have within them the power to change your life and make you an outstanding success no matter what your field. But, only you can make it happen. Only you can provide the spark to make them function. SO. . .as Rich DeVos has said to thousands of audiences all over America. . .

. . . .GET ON WITH IT!!

CHAPTER 3

"REPEAT THEIR LAST FEW WORDS"

Let's continue our quest for lucky profitable sales ideas with the business of communications. After all, a major key tō selling is communicating, and a major key to communicating is this business of listening effectively. Listening not only to what people say, but to what they do not say.

I've discovered a conversation technique that works wonders. Selling is basically the art of answering objections effectively. And the major problem I've encountered is in determining what the real objections are. People have a funny way of clouding up the issue with a lot of false objections. What you have to do is get on a real gut level with them and let it all come out so that you can deal with real issues, real objections. How do you accomplish this?

One thing that makes sense to me is to listen to what people say just before they quit talking. People often quit talking just before they get to what they are really thinking.

In learning the writing craft I've often had instructors tell me to sit down and begin writing, and then after half a dozen pages are completed, to throw away the first page or two. It was positively astounding how many articles and stories could survive without the opening pages. It was as if it took a couple of pages just to get the creative juices flowing. The trouble is, too many people in sales work shut a client up just before he or she is about to deliver the real meat of the problem.

This communications technique is so simple, so easy to put to work immediately that you might doubt its value. Believe me, it will work for you. Here it is. . . .

Simply repeat the last 2 or 3 or 4 or 5 words the other party spoke before they stopped speaking.

For instance, son Daniel comes home, walks right up to me and says, "Dad, I want to use the car tonight."

I repeat the last two words. "Car tonight?"

"Yeah," Dan says, "the guys are going bowling and it is my

Now you'll find out what kind of a salesperson you really are.

turn to drive."

I look up at him questioningly, "Your turn to drive?"

He says, "Well, maybe it isn't my turn but Charlie racked up his dad's car and Tom can't get his and I said you'd let me have out car."

"You said I'd let you have our car?"

I think you get the idea. You can keep the other person talking for a whole month with this technique. But longevity isn't the point. People will tell you things that they really don't want to tell you. They will pour out their souls, but most important, they will reveal to you their real objections and usually a good salesperson can answer those objections effectively and close the sale.

I first discovered this technique having lunch at the Camelback Inn in Scottsdale, Arizona with an author and an agent. The agent was using the technique on the author and he was getting information from this fellow that was so far beyond what this author wanted to reveal that I was stunned. And he was doing it with just a single word or two. The conversation became more and more revealing and later as I studied the events that had transpired I realized that the agent had used a similar technique on me and probably learned more about me in fifteen minutes than most people discover in years.

One word of warning. Save this technique for special occasions. Use it when you get the feeling that someone isn't exactly leveling with you. Or use it when you get a gut feeling that the other party really wants to share more with you but is uncomfortable about getting started.

Try it on your spouse tonight. . . .just repeat the last few words, like. . . ."A headache?"

CHAPTER 4

"MAKING REJECTION WORK FOR YOU"

Let's talk about making rejection work for you. Some people think that rejection is an ugly word. It is a personal put down and it can put you right out of business if you fail to understand it.

Last night I telephoned a friend who is just getting started in the sales profession. She'd encountered a whole week of rejection and was feeling mighty low. She planned to work on Saturday morning, had an appointment, and so I asked her to do a little project of visualization with me. "Now," I suggested, "get comfortable, close your eyes and let us see what will happen tomorrow when you make that call. First of all, picture that couple you'll be calling on. They are out at the location where they just purchased a couch. They are happy with that purchase. Is everything true so far?" "Yes," she said, "they are very pleased. They really need a couple of matching chairs and we happen to have two in stock. That is what the call is all about." "OK," I said. "Now imagine them walking over to the chairs and sitting down. They are smiling. They are happy. They have just purchased the chairs from you. Can you see it? You have the executed contract in your hand. You have completed the sale. Do you see it?" And do you know what she said. . . .she said, "They'll probably want to think it over." POW! I said "You just killed the sale."

"But that is what people have been saying all week, and that is why I haven't sold anything."

That young would-be salesperson was a victim of rejection. She let it cloud her thinking. She had programmed herself to expect rejection and people just wouldn't let her down. She got what she expected. Then we talked about the week before when she had been so successful. She was expecting to sell and she did. I think she understands now.

EVERY once in a while when somebody discovers that I get a lot of my writing published, they ask me how to go about submitting manuscripts. It is really very simple. All you do is take a plain piece of 8½ x 11 bond paper, and you type your name and address in the upper left hand corner. Then skip a few lines and put the title of your piece in the center of the sheet. Then drop a few lines and type "by". . .and you put the name you want to go by. I use Art Fettig.

YOU drop a few more lines and start typing your story or poem or whatever. That's it. Leave plenty of margin all the way around, and on the second page just type 2, and your name at the top, and keep going.

WHEN you finish you just fold the thing into thirds, put it into an envelope and address it to the magazine you want to run it. Be sure to enclose a self-addressed stamped envelope so they can mail you a check. That's all there is to the writing business. Then when the editor gets your story, or poem, or what have you, he types out a check and sends it to you in your envelope.

HERE'S a poem I wrote some time ago, and there is a reason I want you to read it. It's called "Pay Attention Brother."

Do you ever get that winded feeling,
Ever find your head a reeling,
Keepin' up with the Jones' down the street?
Now I want you to pay attention to me.
Did you ever get to feeling gloomy,
Just because they seemed a little more elite?
Well then brother, if you're like me,
You'd like to find a place to flee,
A place where you don't have to be keepin' up.
A place where people smile a lot,
And are quite content with what they've got,
And are grateful that they've got coffee to fill their cup.
To appreciate what you get brother,
That's the secret, there ain't no other,
Just thank God that you've got something nice.
And don't start thinkin' that it's disaster,
When you see the other guy movin' faster,
Count your blessings brother, that's darn good advice.

Well. . .that's enough. . .you get the idea. . .it goes on and on like that for some twenty-six lines.

I wrote that several years ago. And, just as I explained, I typed out the poem. . .folded it, put it in an envelope and included a self-addressed envelope for the check to come back to me.

OOH. I forgot something. I forgot to tell you that sometimes you don't get a check. Sometimes you get back what they call a rejection slip.

AND in this case, the first time I sent this poem out, the editor. . . .I don't know what was wrong with him. . . .but anyway, he didn't send me a check, he sent me a rejection slip.

SO, I just took a couple more envelopes and sent it out again. And would you believe it, I got another rejection slip.

WELL, I knew it was a great work of Art. . . .I'm in the rare position where everything I do is a work of Art. Art Fettig. So I sent the poem out again. And it came back. And I sent it again. . . .and it came back and I sent it again, and again, and again.

I sent that poem out fifteen times, and finally I got a nice letter from the editor of a magazine called Modern Maturity. And she wrote me and said, "Art, we love your poem and we want to use it but we don't pay anything."

WELL by then I was discouraged? I was also running out of postage stamps. So I wrote her and I said, "Fine. You can have the poem, just send me a copy of it when you publish it."

AND then I waited. I waited and I waited and I waited. . . .16 months I waited, and finally I wrote to that gal and I said, "I don't mind giving you my poetry. . . .it doesn't really matter that much about money but if you are going to use my poem then use it and send me a copy, but otherwise send it back."

NOW, that was the wrong thing to say to that gal because she sent it back.

AND I sent that poem to another magazine and it came back . . .and I sent it out again and it came back. . .and again. . .and again. . .and again. . .and again.

FINALLY, the twenty sixth time I sent that poem out I got a letter from the editor of a magazine called Liguorian. . . .and I got a nice check with it.

AND since then that poem has been published three or four times.

TALENTS. I don't know if that particular poem shows any special talent, I do know that audiences seem visably moved when I read it to them. The whole point is that whenever you try to use your particular talents. . . .whenever you try to share your unique talent with others, you often find a wall of rejection.

WHENEVER you attempt to put your talent to work on your particular job you often find resistence. And what most people fail to understand is that this rejection process is necessary. Otherwise there would be no polish on talents. No shine. No glow. Only by trying and failing and getting up again and again can we really grow as human beings.

I have distributed thousands of copies of that poem to people in the sales field. And I encourage them to hang that poem on their office wall. Twenty-six rejections. Very, very personal rejections, and they all hurt, every one of them. But somehow I got up after being knocked down and I got up just one more time than the would-be that failed.

When you feel discouraged, take a look at that poem. . . .not the greatest poem in the world, I'll admit that, but it found a home. Have you tried twenty-five times? How many times did you try to close? Recently I saw some interesting sales statistics that showed that most sales are made after the fifth closing attempt. That the real top salesmen in this country have one thing in common. . . .they know and use a wide variety of closes. Too many would-be salespeople know only one close and they dread using it. "No" means "not-yet," and so the pro's keep adding value and information.

I don't want to break your back with statistics, but here's a set of statistics that can change your selling future. Half the sales people in the world make one call and give up on the prospect. Eighteen percent make two calls. Seven percent make three calls. Five percent make four calls, and get this. . . .20% make five calls or more. And that 20% who overcome rejection and go back five or more times. . . .they account for 80% of the sales made.

Making calls. . . .trying to close, again and again and again. A sales secret? Something new? Not at all. There are really no secrets. . . .just answers people haven't applied yet to succeed.

CHAPTER 5

"TURN ON YOUR SUBCONSCIOUS MIND"

You say you'd like to be more creative? More ingenius? You'd like to change your luck and come up with better ideas and better solutions to your problems? You'd like to put a bit of sparkle into your thinking?

WELL, what would you say if I suggested that quite possibly you've only been using a small part of that wonderful brain of yours effectively? No, I'm not selling that hard stuff that lights your mind up and allows you to see things in triplicate as they drive you off to the funny farm. I'm talking about using the equipment you already have, but using it in a more efficient manner.

PERHAPS you've been working your conscious mind too hard, when if you'd put your subconscious mind to work properly you'd improve your thinking and solve some of life's most perplexing problems.

The majority of creative solutions to problems don't come from conscious thinking. They are the work of the subconscious mind.

FEHR, the French Scientist, made a study of the working habits of his contemporaries and found that 75% of the scientists stated that their important discoveries came to them when they were not actively engaged in research.

MANY creative writers get their best ideas when they are far away from their writing desks. This is heartening to me, because sometimes all I get at my writing table is frustrated.

SO maybe you'll agree that it would be a good thing to let your subconscious do the work while you go out and bowl or sit in your rocking chair or whittle a wooden whistle. But just how do you turn this subconscious critter on?

I'VE conducted my own experiments, and over a period of years I've come up with the following guides that help me. Maybe they'll work for you.

1. Consciously turn your problem over to your sub-

conscious. That means that you must first define your problem. Write it down so that your subconscious will have adequate data to work with. I call this the proper care and feeding of the subconscious mind. Feed it properly and it will grow.

2. Another way to feed your subconscious mind the required data is by discussing the problem with somebody else. Go over all of the pros and cons. All of the data. Then just end the conversation with no decision, no conclusion.

3. Approach each problem with a positive attitude. Act as if you sincerely expect your subconscious to take over. Act as if you expect a good result.

4. Once you've turned your problem over to your subconscious then force yourself to let go of it consciously. Think about something else.

5. Get outside and commune with nature. Take a walk. If you see a tree then pick a leaf and look at it closely. Pick a blade of grass and examine it. Touch a flower if you see one. If there is snow on the ground, pick it up and feel it. I don't understand a lot of the things I do, but if they work, why knock them?

6. Once you've built up some success in using your subconscious mind, tell others about your success. Possibly my subconscious runs on recognition. The nicer I talk about it the better it works.

7. When your subconscious starts to deliver a solution, write it down on paper. Write it down and right away try to expand on the idea with your conscious thinking.

8. When you don't feel a solution surging out of your mind, approach the problem with a positive attitude. I once fed a story problem to my subconscious, and when I woke up the next morning there didn't seem to be a thought in my head. I rolled a piece of paper into my typewriter, put my fingers on the keyboard in happy anticipation and typed out the final thousand words of my story without a bit of hesitation. And all without any real conscious thinking.

9. Always reprogram your subconscious mind just before going to bed. If you must, then talk to yourself. Give your subconscious a nickname. Mine is Whiz. "Whiz," I might say, "I'm counting on you to find a solution to this mess. I know you can do it, Whiz. Now I'm leaving this problem totally in your hands. I'm going to forget it. Understand?" Whiz is a very understanding subconscious. Once we've had our little talk I think more tranquil thoughts and I go to sleep.

10. Don't limit your subconscious thinking to just one subject. Your brain is a marvelous workshop. It can work on a

dozen projects at one time. While your conscious thinking is limited to just your waking hours, your subconscious can go at it twenty-four hours a day. Turn any problem you might have over to your subconscious. It just might keep working on the problem for months and then later, when you've completely forgotten the problem, the solution will pop into your conscious thinking.

DID you ever see the statue of The Thinker? There he sits, day after day, struggling with his conscious mind. I'll just bet you that if that fellow learned how to use his subconscious mind he'd be down at the river having a grand time pulling in fish, while his subconscious mind made him the greatest thinker that ever was.

CHAPTER 6

INTRODUCING

The first time I heard it, it was like music to my ears and believe me, it was a brand new tune that I had never heard before. I had just finished making a complete jack ass out of myself. John Burdakin, then Vice Prisident of Grand Trunk Western Railroad was visiting Battle Creek and when we attended a retirement party, I went to introduce him to my wife Ruth. Frankly, at that time I didn't have all that much experience with railroad vice presidents and I was so scared that I introduced him as John Bandeen. Robert Bandeen was then the new President of Grand Trunk.

He simply smiled, explained to Ruth that his name was John Burdakin and then went on to tell her that he saw a lot of potential in her husband and that the company had every intention of putting my talents to work for the good of the company.

I'd never heard a company official tell anyone about my talents or my potential before, especially to my wife. This was my introduction to part of the style that makes John Burdakin one of the most effective leaders I have ever met.

At future functions I listened as he introduced me to others and I discovered a definite pattern. Whenever he made an introduction he did a little selling job to both parties. It went something like this. . ."Mr. Johnson, meet Art Fettig. Art is doing some exciting things for us in the field of audio visuals. Art. . . this is Tom Johnson. Tom is with the Wyandotte Corporation and I guess he is just about the best salesman I have ever met."

What Mr. Burdakin was doing was a super job of selling one party to another. He took the time to discover at least one outstanding thing about each party and he told you about that item when he made an introduction.

Listen the next time a round of introductions are going on. Listen to what people say. Is it just. . .Dave. . .this is Tom? With just a little effort and planning you can turn the process of making introductions into a really effective means of paying a sincere compliment, or you can really issue a challenge to a party. I've heard Mr. Burdakin introduce a new employee this way. "This is Bernard Watkins, a new member of our marketing team. We're expecting great things from Bernard."

"This is Tom Snyder. . .Tom is the #1 salesman with our company." Now if Tom isn't yet, he'll darn sure make an effort to become #1 in a hurry."

Contrived? Deceptive? No way. When you use this technique it is imperative that you pay sincere compliments. Take the time to find one outstanding thing about everyone you know. Look for the greatness in everyone you meet.

I'll never forget that moment that I really messed up the introduction between my wife Ruth and John Burdakin. He paid me the first genuine compliment that I'd heard in twenty-five years of working for the railroad. And that was the moment that I really started believing in myself.

John Burdakin is the President of Grand Trunk Western Railroad now and in my book his greatest asset is his ability to make people believe in themselves.

CHAPTER 7

"MUTUAL SELLING"

Now I'd like to tell you about a friend of mine named George Duval. That's Duval. . . .D-U-V-A-L. Remember that name, George Duval. George is one of the most dynamic insurance salesmen I've ever met. . .I guess he would be ranked #1 in the three or four adjoining counties. He has been in the Million Dollar Roundtable for sixteen years in a row, and this means he has exceeded one million dollars in sales each year. Last year alone he sold nearly four million dollars worth of insurance. The other day I asked George about his secret.

"IT wasn't always that way," he explains. "When I first came to this town I had no friends. Didn't know a soul. I just had a burning idea that I had something new in insurance and I was going to prove it. I had to prove it first to myself and then to the company I worked for as well. They weren't too sure my idea was sound, and for that reason I worked strictly on commission with no guarantee. That first year I made less than $100 a month. I had a wife and two children to support and the money just wasn't coming in. I met a friend who was just starting out in the health insurance field and he too was an out-of-towner."

"FOR that first year we both nearly starved to death, but both of us kept our heads up high and worked hard every day and we began to tell people we met about each other. Every time we met someone we brought up our friend's name. We made a big point of telling everyone about what a fine future that other guy had. How he was beginning to sell like a house afire. What a tremendous background the other guy had for his particular field. We actually studied each other carefully so that we could really lay it on, but do it truthfully. As we really got into the swing of selling each other to others we began to see our business improve."

"BELIEVE me," George confided, as he winked his friendly confident wink that identifies him, "it is a much nicer thing to do, build somebody up than tear somebody down. People like you and respect you for it. Well, people started to believe in us. Everything we said began to spread among the businessmen in town and as our stature grew, our sales soared. After that first year we were both well on our way to success."

MY friend wasn't telling me the secret to success in the insurance business. He was simply talking about success in living. Whether you are an insurance salesman, a beautician, or a helper in a florist shop, this same secret can aid you in your search for happiness and success. Think about that last conversation you had with someone. Did you mention the name of a third party? Did you say something nice about him, something honest and interesting? Or did you knock somebody? Pass on a little blue gossip? How do you think you impressed that other person?

THERE is an old sales maxim that goes, "Never tear down your competition." It is based on the simple fact that people don't like you if you are always knocking other products or other people. Just not mentioning others isn't much fun either. The real joy in life lies in selling your friends and their talents to other people.

AFTER listening to George, I started thinking a little bit about our conversations in the past. I realized that every time we had talked, he had talked favorably about at least one other individual. Not just casually mentioning him, but giving me the the whole pitch about what a fine guy, what a tremendous success, what an asset to the community, so and so was.

THEN I recalled how my friend was always selling me to others. Introducing me as a fine author. A creative genius. A man that was going up-up-up. I started remembering my conversations with others, about how I had unconsciously brought up the subject of my insurance friend and his exceptional qualifications. Hardly a day passed that I wasn't telling someone about my insurance friend and his vast knowledge.

IT was contagious. Unconscious and contagious. I told my friend about my thoughts, how I was selling him and he was out selling me every day.

"YES", he admitted, "I do it unconsciously now. There are a dozen friends I have whom I sell for every day. And I suppose that somewhere they are out there selling for us, too. It's that simple. It has to be honest selling, your friends have to be a good product or it doesn't work, but when it works it works so well it is unbelievable. I'd really rather be saying something sincerely nice about someone anyway."

AFTER our conversation I suddenly remembered a couple of unexpected writing assignments that had come my way. By the process of elimination I was easily able to trace those assignments directly to my friend's selling.

WHY don't you work a word of praise about a friend into your daily conversation. Word of mouth advertising is the best in the world, and if you have a friend that deserves praise, then pass it around. Do your work so that it deserves praise and soon your friends will catch the habit. It's contagious, and believe me, it is one of the nicest things in world to catch.

MAYBE luck and success comes to the guy who helps himself, but it comes even faster to the person who helps his friends.

Now you remember that name, Duval, George Duval. One of the greatest insurance pension people in the world. And I'll just bet that somewhere right now George Duval is out there selling Art Fettig.

CHAPTER 8

MOVE AROUND

One of the most rewarding ideas I ever picked up came from my sometimes partner and full time great friend, Herb True, America's Greatest Educ-tainer. We were attending a three day meeting and as we arrived, Herb told me the ground rules. "I love you Art, and I love being with you, but we get to spend a lot of time with each other. We both came to this convention to learn as much as we possibly can and we will have a lot of opportunities to learn from one another in the future, but the greatest way that I have learned to get the full benefit from a meeting or convention is to move around and talk with as many people as possible."

He showed the program and some of the sessions he had checked off that he wanted to attend. "There certainly is an impressive list of speakers here and we will both learn a great deal from them, but remember Art, if you let those speakers serve as springboards for ideas and then discuss those ideas with fellow attendees, you will learn that they have a wealth of personal experience to share with you. All you have to do is ask."

Since Herb gave me that idea I have attended dozens of conventions and I have discovered that if I move around and meet new people at every session I soon learn who the real professionals are, and I get their names and when I follow up with them with a letter after the convention then I form lasting friendships with the real experts in every field.

Now, when I encounter a problem in any area, I have a list of experts who will share their knowledge with me for the price of a phone call. Oh yes, there is one other thing. . .I often get calls from them and I feel honored when they ask about my personal experience in a given area.

Recently I talked with a group of 600 and I was the wrap up speaker for the 3 day session. I asked the audience how many of them were sitting next to the people they came with. . .not their spouses, but other people that they work with every day. There

ART
FETTIG
Mr.
LUCKY

must have been over 550 hands raised. Then I asked them how many of them had attended meetings without the people that they work with every day, and I saw only a half a dozen hands. The sad fact was that those people had missed one of the greatest educational experiences of their lives. Sharing ideas and experience with people from other locations who are in the same line of work.

At the next meeting, the program chairman told me that he had a new idea that he planned to put to use. "Next time," he explained, "we will have personalized business cards printed for every attendee. Then at the first session we plan to explain how important it is that they move around and meet each other and share ideas. We will give them each a hundred business cards and encourage them to move around after each session and get to know other people with similar interests. Then we hope to encourage them to correspond with each other and share new ideas and techniques. That way they can benefit from a rewarding learning experience all year long."

When I finished my talk one elderly lady came up to me and explained that she would be attending a meeting in a month and that she planned to shake hands with every person at that convention. "I thought that all the talent was on the stage but now, for the first time I realize that the formal program is just a tiny part of what can happen. I'm sure that with a bit of experience I will learn to find the most intelligent people there and pick up a wealth of learning."

In every session there is one who is the best at his job and there is one who is worst. And believe me, you can learn from all of them. Don't feel obligated to stay with any group. Move around. And don't be afraid to walk up and join a discussion. The braver you become the more chances you have for getting just some of the learning that is available at every meeting you attend.

Now when Herb True and I travel to sessions together we set up meeting times where we quickly share some of the great ideas we have discovered. We do spend a bit of time together, but mostly we move around and enjoy every minute of it.

CHAPTER 9

"THE NINE MOST IMPORTANT WORDS"

WHAT are the nine most important words in the English language? Money. . .love. . .sex. . .health. . .I don't know what they are. I do know what the 17 most persuasive words are and we'll get to those in a later chapter. But I've discovered a sentence that is nine words long and to me it has become the most effective combination of nine words I've ever encountered. If I had to isolate the one reason why I have doubled my income in the past year it is this one sentence. Somehow this sentence brings the immediate action I desire in others. It is a magic key to the love instinct in others. It compels people to do things they wouldn't ordinarily do for you. Are you ready?

WELL hold off for a minute. Let me tell you a bit about myself. I'm a writer. First I was a writer. Then I discovered photographs to illustrate my articles. From that I progressed on to producing slide shows. You know, 35mm slides, together with taped sound tracks. And then the next thing I started was writing speeches for corporate executives and finally for some professional speakers. I went to Chicago for a week with a speaker and worked the whole time writing special material for his performance. I must have written 15 things for him and he used just one. I decided that the following year I would return to that meeting, somehow get on the program and launch my career as a professional speaker. Well, I did it. I had nine minutes on the program. Several people have told me that I was voted the top speaker that year and I booked nearly $5,000 worth of speaking engagements in that nine minutes. My speaking career was launched that day on a national basis. Well, it is a great life, traveling around the country giving speeches, but it is also time consuming, and I still do a lot of audio-visual work. One day I made the amazing discovery that I could make a lot more money if I could cut down my travel time. I studied my bookings and learned that I really wasn't getting much work near my home. What I realized was that I was probably better known in Dallas and Miami than I was 20 miles from home. I was one of the best kept secrets in the State of Michigan. That was my problem.

How to get better known near home.

NOW I'll tell you those Nine Most Important Words In The English Language and how they work for me. The words are. . . "I've got a problem and I need your help." You thought they'd be more complicated, didn't you? No, just, "I've got a problem and I need your help." And every time I talk to an audience in Michigan I tell this story, and every time I finish a talk I go up to the fellow who hired me and I say, "I've got a problem and I need your help. My problem is that I'm not all that well known in Michigan and I want to do more meetings here. You can help me. If you are satisfied that I did a good job for you I want you to mail three copies of my brochure to three other meeting planners that you know in Michigan, along with your recommendation." I always give them four brochures and then I ask for a return booking. Nine words. "I've got a problem and I need your help." It changed my luck. Tripled my Michigan bookings.

I used the same sentence the other day in a letter to a man in Senior Management. He has pulled out all of the stops in helping me solve my problem. I've had a dozen letters from people who have had outstanding success using this simple technique.

NOW, while I have your attention, I have this problem and I need your help. Would you tell your program chairman that you'd like to have Art Fettig at your next big meeting? That is Fettig. . .no "n" in the last name. . . F E T T I G.

CHAPTER 10

"HIGH PRESSURE SALES"

THE modern salesman uses high pressure salesmanship just once each day. After that it isn't necessary. Know when he uses it? First thing each morning. He sells himself first on himself and then on his product. That's right, he sells himself on the idea that he can and will do a good job that day and then he sells himself on his product.

IF he is a really good salesman he goes over his product's best points. Sure he knows them. He knows them in his sleep but by reviewing them he can renew his enthusiasm for that product.

WHEN a salesman truly believes in himself and his product there is absolutely nothing that can stand in his way of success. When a salesman questions his own ability or the quality of his product, nothing will help him succeed. He's lost. He might make an occasional sale here and there, but I'm talking about success. Real success. Continued growing success. If you find you've lost faith in your product then get rid of it. Get hold of something you believe in.

YOUR product won't always have to be the best and greatest on the market, but the important thing is that you sell yourself on it's good points. Sell yourself on the major reasons the customer should buy. Sell yourself and believe yourself and then believe in yourself and your ability.

DID you ever watch a con man work? A good con man? Well, did you ever watch an actor portray a good con man in action? Do you know the secret of a good con man's success? He believes. That's right, he believes in what he is selling. Now you know and I know that the con man is wrong. He's dead wrong, and I am not suggesting that you take on the qualities of a con man. What I am suggesting is that you learn a lesson from the con man. B E L I E V E. The con man believes in himself and he forces himself to believe in his product.

REMEMBER that magnificent musical "The Music Man?" Remember Harold Hill, the con man who peddled musical instruments? Remember the belief and enthusiasm he put into his pitch when he said "RIVER CITY IS GOING TO HAVE A BAND?" Harold Hill believed. Now what made Harold Hill a con man was the fact that he didn't clutter up his mind with the realization that what he believed in was impossible. He believed that River City could have a band with 76 trombones leading the big parade, and when Harold Hill believed, the whole darn town of River City believed, and Harold Hill sold more darned musical instruments than anyone would have believed.

HAROLD HILL only high-pressured one person. Himself. He did such a good job that his unharnassed enthusiasm did the major selling job for him.

DON'T be a con man but do be a believer. When you start shaving or fussing up in the morning, start in there with the hard sell. Give that guy in the mirror the full load and don't let up until you've got that human all fired up and rarin' to go. Don't stop with your spiel until that person believes it is the best product in the world, and further, that you are the only really qualified person around to sell that product. Got it? Got yourself fired up? OK, now turn yourself loose and you just meet up with that person again tonight after a day's work and see if you didn't do all you told yourself you could.

CHAPTER 11

"GET OUT OF STEP"

Any of you who has ever gone into battle remembers that before each attack there is this thing that is very much like a sales meeting. It is similar to the kick off for a United Way Campaign. The Colonel, or whatever rank of officer they could persuade to come up that close to the front line, addresses the troops. He gives a real sales talk about how you're breaking the enemies' back . . . how this one hill you are about to attack just might make the difference between a world full of slave-ridden communism or fun loving democracy . . . it is a real heartrending experience and he really fires you up. It was November, 1951, and we were just about to attack this hill in Korea called Old Baldy . . . again. Like a ping pong ball this hill kept goin' back and forth, and this Colonel we called Ring Mount Dan, came up and gave us the traditional speech. They called him Ring Mount because it seems he wasn't exactly number one on the men's charts, and someone had tried to do old Ring Mount Dan in, so now whenever he drove up to give us a pep talk, he had a jeep with a 50 MM machine gun mounted on a ring, and a sergeant would keep that gun trained on us while the Colonel talked. Heck, I didn't think he was that bad a speaker.

SO after the speech we took showers and shaved and got new uniforms so that the enemy would believe we were fresh troops and then right after that we attacked. There we were, charging up Old Baldy yellin' "Remember the Little Big Horn." And those yellow devils remembered. Well, we upheld the tradition of General Custer's old outfit the Seventh Regiment of the First Cavalry Division. We were wiped out.

A lot of people seem to have a morbid curiosity about how people were wounded in the service. In my particular case, I was running straight up Old Baldy carrying a couple of cans of Machine Gun Ammo, and this mortar went all over the place and I stopped some of it. I got hit at the front . . . . . in the rear.

AND some people are unkind. When they find out that I was hit in the rear they make fun of me. They laugh and make cracks like . . . "Fettig's got lead in his fanny." "Fettig's got lead in his fanny." And you know something? I don't mind this. I don't care about the kidding. They can go on forever making fun of the fact that I got hit in the rear end. I'm darn happy about the whole thing. In fact, every night I get down on my hands and knees and thank God that I wasn't turned the other way. You know . . . I could be signing soprano in a boy's choir right now.

AFTER that attack we were taken to a hospital . . . most of us . . . and we took the hill that day, I understand, but it was a bloody event, and right after that they declared our entire Division "Combat Ineffective." We were wiped out. And they transferred our Unit to Hokkaido, Japan. It was terrible. All of our officers had been wounded, and we actually ended up the day with no commissioned officers left. In fact, we had a supply sergeant who was serving as the company commander.

After a couple of months in the hospital I reported to my old company . . . Able Company, First Battalion, Seventh Regiment . . . and I was assigned back to my rifle squad. Only things had changed. We had all new people in our outfit. What they had done was activate the Tennessee National Guard, and our outfit was just loaded with young inexperienced kids who were just loaded with rank. We had a Sergeant Major . . . a Sergeant Major . . . that's the old Army Guy who is loaded with experience and really runs things. Our Sergeant Major . . .was a kid nineteen years old who had never seen any action except in the back of a bar one night in Tennessee.

A bunch of National Guard kids running around with stripes all over their arms. We found out that most of these kids had made their rank in the Cub Scouts, and then when they joined the Guard they let them keep it.

IT was awful. All of the privates had tasted months of bitter combat, and because of all of the fighting and confusion, none had been promoted, and here we were being led by a lot of kids who knew nothing but playing field maneuvers on weekends in the woods back home.

AND to make matters worse, the Army picked our unit to attempt a new style of integration. They had split up the all black units in the Army and were attempting to assign the black non-commissioned officers to units throughout the Army. Just happened, our platoon landed a Staff Sergeant by the name of

Sergeant Crass. And he had a dream. And his dream was to turn us into the best drill team in the Far East Command.

NOW any of you who has ever done any kind of drilling knows that the only way you get to be the best drill team in the Far East Command is to drill and to drill and to drill.

SERGEANT Crass had us out there marchin' . . . marchin' . . . marchin'. He had us out there marchin' day and night.

NOW most of us just weren't natural born marchers. I mean, the sun for us didn't really set on the spirit of Hup, Hope, Hip Four. In fact, it wasn't too long at all until we were all pretty darned bored with the whole thing.

NOW when Sergeant Crass saw we were losin' interest he introduced us to what they call the "Jodie Cadences". Maybe you've heard them. Maybe you heard different ones than I'm gonna tell you about. But the Jodie Cadences are a kind of chant and the Sergeant would call out these rhymes and we would march in time to them and learn some replies that we shouted together. They went something like this.

Hey, ain't no use in goin' home,

Old Jodie's got your gal and gone.

Ain't no use in goin' back,

Cause Jodie's stole your Cadillac.

So sound off!

ONE, TWO,

Once more!

THREE, FOUR,

CADENCE COUNT!

ONE, TWO, THREE, FOUR, ONE, TWO. . .THREE FOUR.

You had a good home but you left

YOUR RIGHT!

Jodie was there when you left

YOUR RIGHT!

So sound off!

ONE, TWO,

Once more!

THREE, FOUR.

Goin' back home today,

YOUR RIGHT!

See my moosamae

Yeah, Yeah

Tell that gal I've gone

Yeah, Yeah

Far Far Way From Home

THAT'S RIGHT

Do you want to go?

YOU'RE RIGHT.

Do you want to go?

YOU'RE RIGHT.

Then sound off . . .

ONE, TWO

Once more!

THREE, FOUR.

He had us out there drillin' and shoutin' . . . marchin' . . . marchin' . . . day and night . . . night and day . . .

AND then he started getting fancy . . . He started calling out stuff like . . .

DOUBLE to the rear to the right flank march . . . double to the rear to the left flank march . . . SQUAD . . . column left DO IT

AND WE DID IT!

IT was horrible . . . hour after hour . . . marchin', marchin', marchin'.

AND all of a sudden it dawned on me . . . "Fettig, you aren't doin' your own thing."

NOW all my life I've been preachin' about the importance of being an individual. About being yourself. About stepping out from the crowd and being unique, and there I was with everybody else doing . . . your left . . . your left . . . your left.

NOW in the Army they've got this thing they call the "Change

Step." All it is, is a little skip. You just give a little skip and all of a sudden you're marchin' along by yourself.

AND this old Sergeant had us out there for hours and he was goin' YOUR LEFT, YOUR LEFT . . . and I just gave it a little skip and there I was marchin' to my own beat.

WELL, he has a pretty good eye and right away he noticed that I'm not in step and so he yells, "Fettig, get in step. Fettig, get in step."

YOUR LEFT. YOUR LEFT . . .

AND I just kept doing it my way and I was thinkin', "That's right, baby, that's right."

AND he looks right at me and screams, "Fettig, get in step." And I just kept ignoring him and kept a doin' my own thing.

WELL now this guy wasn't the dumbest thing that ever walked, so he takes a good deep breath and yells out . . . "Everybody but Fettig, change step MARCH." And every body but me gives this little skip and now all of a sudden we're all marchin' along together.

ONLY now they are doin' my thing. Now they are all marchin' to my drum. And you know . . . just then for a minute the Army wasn't such a horrible thing.

SOMETIMES, if you want to be you, it is necessary for you to skip. To get out of step.

MAYBE Henry David Thoreau explained this best when he wrote, "Why should we be in such desperate haste to succeed and in such desperate enterprises? If a man does not keep pace with his companions, perhaps it is because he hears a different drummer. Let him step to the music which he hears, however measured or far away."

LUCKY people have the courage to step out.

CHAPTER 12

"SELL A LITTLE BIT OF YOU"

ONE of the most important sales lessons I ever learned came by talking about the weather. I was just fourteen years old and working as a combination stock boy/salesman part-time in a local shoe store. My employer was a wise old gentleman named W. C. Thompson, and in the shoe business there is a saying that "women don't buy shoes when it's raining outside." "They just come in to look and get out of the rain."

I'D heard the saying, and one rainy day Mr. Thompson called me aside and said, "Art, maybe you've heard that rumor about women and rainy days, but I want you to know that a real salesman sells a lot of shoes on rainy days. He has a captive customer and if you keep on pitching you are bound to sell something."

WELL, it was raining outside and in walked a lady that was well known to all of us. She had a habit of coming in at least once a week and she'd try on a dozen different shoes every time. The only thing wrong was that she never bought a thing. Nothing. No one had ever sold her a dime's worth of merchandise, and even Mr. Thompson, who in my mind was a master salesman, struck out with this lady. It got so that all of the other salesmen would rush to the back of the store when they saw her coming, and since I was the youngest man and first out on the floor I got her.

FIRST I showed her a dozen different shoes, helped her try them on, treated her with extra courtesy. Then as the rain continued, I moved on to our other merchandise.

I showed her shoes for her children, shoes for her husband, in fact I went through out entire line. Then I went on to women's hose, mens stockings, arch supports, shoe polish, and finally as the rain was letting up I got to the shoe laces. The rain had just about stopped when she broke down and bought a ten cent pair of shoe laces. I was jubilant as I rang up the sale. It wasn't such a big victory but at least I'd cracked her shell.

THE following day this same lady returned with her husband and children and I sold every member of her family two pairs of shoes. It was the largest single sale I'd ever made in that store.

A few weeks later we put in a supply of umbrellas, and from that time on we seldom let a shopper get out of our store on a rainy day without making some sale. My sale reminded the other men that you don't make sales unless you make presentations.

RECENTLY I had the opportunity to attend a sales meeting of encyclopedia salesmen. The Christmas season had just passed and I had the chance to talk to a number of the men individually. A few told me that of course they hadn't sold much because it was the Christmas season. "People are out of town." "They are busy trimming the tree." "They've spent all of their money on gifts." "They don't want to be bothered." These were the low production boys with the excuses.

THEN I talked to some of the key sellers. "Christmas is the best time of all. People are in the habit of spending and it isn't so difficult to get them to turn loose of a dollar." "People feel more obligated to their children during this season and it makes them more eager to listen to a talk on child education." "It's near the end of the year and they take inventory of what they've put off all year. It's a great time to sell."

IF you talk to people who are failing they'll tell you that times are bad. We're in a recession. People are hanging onto their money.

IF you talk to the producer, he'll tell you that this is the greatest time in our history.

THE rain, the season, the financial climate are all important and they truly affect a client and his behavior. But more than anything else, it is you that is important in how you produce. It is how you react to each thing that counts. Every single thing that happens can be an asset or a liability. A wall or a stepping stone.

THAT old saying, "If they give you a lemon, make lemonade" is more important today than ever before. We seem to be going through a negative attitude era. People are discontent with the government, with taxes, and crime and drugs and pollution, and it is easy to fall in with the negative crowd. It is easy to feel that every day is a rainy day and that people don't buy when it's raining. But once again, whenever my chin isn't quite as high as it should be, I think about W. C. Thompson and what he told me that rainy day many years ago. "A real salesman sells a lot of shoes on a rainy day."

HOW about you? How is your attitude? Are you able to put your finger on what's bothering you? Can you spot a problem and study it? Can you say this to yourself, "How can I turn this into an asset instead of a liability? How can I make this situation work for me?"

ONCE you learn to recognize problems you'll find it a lot easier to answer objections. When a client throws a negative objection at you, you should learn to say, "That's all the more reason you should buy." Everything can be turned into a positive asset if only you learn to see it.

I'VE come to believe that there are only two kinds of people in the world. Positive and Negative. The negative ones walk around with a great big minus sign stamped on their foreheads. You can spot them in a minute. "That won't work. I wouldn't try that. No use in doing that." And you can also spot them from the position they've reached in life. The positive people wear a smile and a huge plus sign written across their face. It says, "I think I can. I'll try it. Why not." And those people with the positive attitude go out and sell when it's raining and they sell when it's snowing and when times are good and when times are bad and during the Christmas season and golf season and football season and in every other season. And it isn't so much the weather that makes the difference. It's the whether that is important. Whether you try. Whether you make the necessary effort. Whether you believe in yourself and your product.

AND that's the lucky lesson that I learned as a fourteen-year-old part-time stock boy/salesman. That a real salesman sells when the sun is shining, but he sells even more when it's pouring outside.

CHAPTER 13

"FEEL GOOD ABOUT YOURSELF"

LAST week my wife, Ruth, and I were sitting with a small group of people on a beach in Barbados, British West Indies, spending some of the money I'd made in selling. It was raining and we were sitting under one of those straw beach umbrellas. Rain in Barbados is a pleasant event; it lasts only a few moments and it is rather refreshing. As we sat there, a native boy came running up with his arms full of woven hats, mats and purses. "You lucky people have been just waiting here for me," he announced excitedly. Then he proceeded to do the darndest selling job I've seen in years.

COMPETITION on the beaches is really rough, and we talked to the young lad about selling after he'd loaded us all up on straw goods. "Sure, there are lots of other boys selling on the beaches, but I outsell them all because I am a master salesman." He explained. "I don't ask people if they want to buy. I know they want to buy and I know they want to buy from me."

ONE of the gals asked him if it wasn't because he had superior merchandise. He looked down at the things he'd sold us and smiled. "Merchandise has nothing to do with selling," he said. "It's how you feel about what you have. I believe that what I have to sell is exactly what you want to buy. I could buy better items, but the price would be higher. This way you overlook a few flaws in my hats and you think about what a bargain you are getting. Besides, the sun is hot and what better place to sell a cool, shady hat?"

I watched the boy as he ran to the next group of people, and I overheard him as he started his pitch. "You folks have been just waiting for me," he said. Again and again he repeated it, and again and again he sold those people. He was right. Absolutely right. Those people were just waiting for him, and people all over the world are just waiting for a master salesman to call on them and show them what they have to sell.

WHAT about you? How do you approach a prospect? Do you feel that you are imposing? Are you apologetic? Are you

YOU LUCKY PEOPLE HAVE JUST BEEN WAITING FOR ME!!

excited about your product? Do you really believe that you have something which would benefit the prospect, or are you just pushing something that you have little faith in? What you are depends a great deal on what you believe you are.

A sales executive who was sitting under our beach umbrella laughed at the boy as he rushed down the beach. "You know," he said, "I bet if you gave that kid a load of Hoover Vacuum Cleaners and sent him down the beach with them he'd really clean up." It was his joke. At least, with the sun peeking out from under that passing rain cloud, and the beauty of the sea, and those tall icy refreshments that were coming every half hour, it seemed like a very funny joke, and yet, like most good jokes, it was based on truth. You could give that young man almost any product and he'd clean up with it. The key to his success lay in just a few of the words he said. "I am a master salesman." He was absolutely sold on that idea.

IN our city we have a father and son general insurance team. On all of their advertising they use two words to describe their qualifications. "The Professionals." And that would be an excellent description of that young native boy going barefoot along those relaxing West Indies beaches in Barbados.

AND why is it that so many young men go out with a product or a service to sell and come back in a week or a month, and turn the product in and say, "It just won't sell." Oh, they say other things too. "Money is too tight." "The competition has our price beat." "People are afraid to open their doors to strangers now days." "I can make more money working by the hour than on commission."

WHY is it that it is a rare individual who can go out and really make the big money quickly in the direct sales field? Again it is a simple fact. Most new people lack confidence. They lack the attitude and confidence of a professional.

AS we sat there wiggling our toes in that magic warmth of the sand, I listened to the objections we threw that young man's way. "They are cheaper in town." "I won't be able to pack them." "The hats are for women and I'm a man." "The price is too high." "I don't have my money with me." "I'd rather shop around." The same objections. The same excuses were being tossed at this young man that are being tossed at every salesman all over the world every day, and that young man took each objection and turned it into a sales asset.

HE reminded us of the high taxi fare to town to shop. He rolled up the hats to show how they pack; offered a tiny discount for a large purchase; pointed to a successful banker nearby who was wearing one of his hats. "He looks like a native, not feminine." About money, he'd walk to our rooms with us to get the money. He answered every objection with tact and good humor and he did this because he was prepared for every objection. And from the moment he approached us he began to close the sale. He sold one, then another, then more to each of us and he kept closing as he continued. And once he knew he had extracted the last ounce of tribute, he laughed with us, complimented our good humor and good taste and ran to the next group of waiting customers.

AND so it is all over the world. With people of all ages, of all backgrounds. Yes, with people in far away places and with people in your own neighborhood it is exactly the same. People are willing and waiting to buy a good product for a good price or even just a fair product for a fair price, but they are willing to buy it only from a master salesman.

ARE you that person? Are you a master salesperson? Are you a pro? Are you ready to face the world and say bravely, "You people have just been waiting for me and my product, my service." Can you walk proudly down the street and smile at all you meet and announce, "I'm a master salesperson and you've been waiting for me."

AND on down the beach the young man walked, and his load got lighter and lighter as he sold his products, and on the sand he left a path of footprints, and on the beaches he left a trail of satisfied customers. And under our umbrella he left a message for us and for lucky salespeople all over the world. A message about selling and success. "It's how you feel about yourself and what you have." How do you feel? Are you truly one of THE PROFESSIONALS?

CHAPTER 14

"DARE TO FEAR BUT DO NOT FEAR TO DARE"

"THE only thing we have to fear is fear itself." These were the words of President Franklin D. Roosevelt in his inaugural address to the nation in 1933. Fear and panic practically destroyed the American Free enterprise system when the stock market crashed, and by identifying fear, President Roosevelt hoped to rebuild the nation.

PUTTING fear to work for you can get you tremendous results. But, when you let fear take the driver's seat you can destroy yourself financially, physically and mentally.

MOST people can stand reality no matter how rough the blows fall. It's not what really happens that gets you down, it's what you fear might happen. Perhaps if we better understand fear we can better put it to work for us.

FEAR is an emotion, a painful emotion excited by a sense of impending danger or evil, whether for one's self or for another. An emotion. And an emotion is an agitation or disturbance of the mind. Fear is a mental thing, and if we allow it to take control, our imagination can run away with us and destroy our sense of proportion.

OFTEN, through fear, we build mountains out of mere anthills. We make a very big deal out of a small incident. A noise. A shadow. Or maybe just silence and the lack of a shadow. Fear doesn't need much to work on, it can be a magic multiplier that takes a few unrelated facts and combines them into a sinister affair.

THE human mind is much like a computer, and when you feed your mind fear thoughts, it goes to work and influences your whole system. It works on your heart and you feel your heart pounding, you feel the sweat running down your forehead. It works on all of your senses, and once you begin to realize how fear works you can put it to work for you.

OUR combat troops in Viet Nam were taught to use fear as a survival weapon. The world's greatest entertainers use fear to make their performances sharper. You too can put fear to work for you, and here are ten ways that might start you out:

1. Fear causes excitement. If you want to make a point or increase interest, get excited. Realize that when you have fear just before you attempt something important, it is not a bad thing. It is natural. And welcome that fear as an asset. Let it excite you and use that excitement to increase your enthusiasm.

2. Fear makes you agile. You can run faster when you're really scared. Run faster and leap higher. I once had a vicious dog chase me and I made it over a six foot wall without a strain.

3. Fear gives you added energy. Your endurance can often be doubled if you have fear working for you. Mothers, fearing the safety of their children, have been known to achieve unbelievable feats of endurance.

4. Fear sharpens your senses. Your sense of smell increases. Your sense of touch. A combat rifleman can often sense the presence of an enemy when fear is present.

5. Fear helps you understand your imagination. When you observe another person in a state of panic over an imagined problem it gives you insight into your own imagination. Your imagination is a wonderful asset, but learn how it works so that it doesn't destroy you.

6. Fear makes you prepare. Most disasters can be handled if only people would take the time to do a little preparation. Fear of fire motivates people to plan ahead, and when fire strikes they are ready with a smoke warning alarm, an extinguisher and a safe escape route for their family.

7. Fear makes you consider options. People who suffer from channel vision are often persuaded to look at the other guy's point of view when they are faced with a situation that puts fear into their lives. In a moment of stress you can often start considering alternatives that you blindly refused to look at when you were much calmer.

8. Fear can be a warning signal that you aren't adequately prepared for what you propose. If you truly dread making a certain sales presentation, take a good look at what you're doing. Maybe you should spend more time getting ready, and when you do you'll discover that fear has been replaced by a good helping of enthusiastic excitement.

9. Fear makes you Dare. Often people will reach out and commit themselves to a project when they have a little fear to work with. The silent majority can become a very verbal group when something threatens their safety or the safety of their loved ones.

10. Fear can provide confidence. Many professional entertainers will tell you, "If I'm not nervous before a performance it scares me. I need that extra nervous energy, and if it isn't there, I have to try a lot harder to win an audience."

THERE you have them. Ten ways to put fear to work for you. Can't you find at least ten more ways to put fear to work for you, in your own job?

WHAT about using your knowledge of fear to help others in solving their own problems? How many sales devices are planned strictly on the basis of fear? Putting new fears into the thinking of the client. Fears like, "Tomorrow, might be too late for you to provide for your loved ones."

LEARN to live with fear. Try to understand it. And put fear to work for you for greater success.

FRANKLIN D. Roosevelt put an entire nation back on its feet by giving his people a little better understanding of fear. "The only thing we have to fear is fear itself." Remember those words as you face fear with greater courage and understanding.

F.D.R.

CHAPTER 15

SELL ONE THING AT A TIME

From a used car dealer on a corner lot with just 4 cars to one of the largest, most successful Recreation Vehicle Dealers in Midwest Michigan in just ten years. That is the story of my friend George Ewing, and when I asked him for the one idea that spelled his success George reminded me of a used car that he sold me. "Do you remember that deal, Art?", he asked. "You said you wanted a low mileage Chevy. . .stick shift. . .a six cylinder. . .tudor. . .and I sold you a Ford V-8 Four door that I had on the lot." I remembered and it was the best car buy I ever made. "I listened to what you were saying to me and in my mind I thought about the use you would be making of that car. I saw you driving that Ford I had ready to deliver. And then I concentrated on that one thing. Selling you that car. I remember how you wanted to go down the line and get in every car in my lot and how amazed you were when I wouldn't let you do that. I kept you in that one car." George gave me that warm friendly smile that is his trademark. "That, my friend, is the secret of my success. Selling just one thing at a time. Listening very very hard to a customer before you show him anything. Then matching up his desires with what you have that will fulfill those needs and desires and then concentrating on just one thing. . .getting my product and your needs teamed up together."

George invited me to take a look at his lot. Dozens and dozens of recreation vehicles. Every size and color you could imagine.

"Just look around you, Art. And remember what happened the other day when we went out to lunch together. The waitress handed us a menu with a dozen items on it. Remember? The restaurant was packed and she was busier than a one armed paper hanger with hives, and remember what she said. "The Swiss Steak is really great today." And do you remember what we ate? Swiss Steak. Now we might have messed around with that menu for ten minutes but she helped us make a decision in a hurry. Now in our business, it isn't so much a matter of time. It is just that we've discovered that spending half a day with a customer doesn't necessarily result in a sale. It generally results in a misery of choices for a customer to make and all too often simply results in a confused, would be buyer, walking away without buying because he is so mixed up about what he wants that he cannot make a decision.

I try very hard to talk to a customer before showing him anything. Since trailers are nearly always bought by couples, I try to get the man and his wife together as soon as possible. Quite often the man shops around, but it is the wife that makes the decision. I want to know as much as I can about the couple, and what they really want and need. Then I show them. And that is what I try to teach my sales people. When I first went into the used car business I had to sell what was on my lot. If a customer walked in, it was usually because he saw something that appealed to him. Then, as I got more and more cars in stock to choose from, I discovered that for a while my sales weren't increasing, I was just spending more time with people showing them everything I had. It was sort of a parade. . .we started at one end of the line. . .looked at every car in turn and then when they got to the end of the line they kept right on going to somebody else's lot to continue the game."

I remember how George was involved for a while with the P.T.A. "Same thing there," George explained. "When you want' to sell an idea then stick with that one idea. Don't scatter your presentation. Key in one thing at a time. Sometimes a salesman comes into my office with a big catalog and a dozen different things, and he wonders why he never sells anything. Usually the problem is that he is so busy selling everything that he winds up selling nothing. We concentrate on one customer at a time. . .we find out what he wants a recreation vehicle for, and then we do our best to match him up with the best product we can find."

That is a simple idea and yet when you spend a few hours around George's showroom you will discover that his customers stay sold. They come back again and again and they bring their friends with them.

How about you? I didn't bring George and his business techniques up so that you will build up a recreation vehicle business or a used car lot. We are talking about successful communications in any area. Work on one thing at a time. Present one idea at a time. Work on it. When people try to take you into a different area. . .when they try to take you down the line from one thing to another. . .stop them. Get them back to that one idea you are selling. Then after you have closed the sale. . .then and only then can you move on to the next thing.

George Ewing has built a successful, rapidly growing business on that one idea. Avoid that misery of choice. Stick to one thing. One idea at a time. . .one product. . .and sell it.

CHAPTER 16

"USE YOUR LUCKY CIRCLE OF INFLUENCE"

RECENTLY I asked a friend, who had gone into the soap business, how he was doing with sales. He smiled and answered, "Relatively speaking, I'm doing fine." Well, after a bit of discussion I learned that what he meant by his reply was that he was selling to his relatives. And when I asked him how many sales had come from others as a result of the sales to his relatives, he admitted "none". When I suggested that he hadn't really sold his product to his relatives, but had simply collected a sort of kinship debt, he looked offended. And when I further suggested that he go back to everyone that had bought, and spend some time demonstrating how the product worked, and how great it really was, he felt I was wasting his time. But I persisted and he did go back, and then later when I saw him he proudly told me how those relatives of his had become excited about his fine product and their excitement had generated a whole string of new sales to the friends of his relatives. "Your lucky circle of influence went to work for you," I explained.

HOW is your lucky circle of influence? Does it work for you every day? Do each of your sales generate new prospects?

MAYBE like me, you once explored the life insurance sales field. If so, perhaps you recall writing down the names and addresses of all of your close friends and relatives? And do you remember how offended you felt when your sales manager suggested that this was your list of prospects? It didn't seem just right that you should impose. You expected to be selling life insurance to some other guy. Some guy you'd meet at a country club or something. And then as you became more and more acquainted with your product and more and more convinced that it was a terrific item, you realized that you wanted to sell your friends and relatives because you believed in what you were doing. No doubt, as you began to sell, you saw that your prospect list was growing. If you became a real pro then your circle of influence kept working for you. Because, if you really sold a prospect, then you soon moved into his circle of influence and encompassed the unique circle of influence of all his friends too. And then what happened? What happened to you? Did you grow with your circle, or did you run so fast with your prospecting that you somehow forgot to put in those study hours to qualify you as a real pro? If so, then your circle became less and less influential.

TAKE a look at what you're doing. And take a look at where your success is coming from. Do you see the circle of influence? Can you identify it? Do you recognize how success breeds success and how sales lay the ground work for more sales? And if you're not content with your achievement then sit down and think about how you can extend your lucky circle of influence. One way is to prospect for prospectors. Take a look at the list of satisfied customers you've amassed. How many of them are specialists in their own particular field? How many are outstanding? Make a list of those who are the best in their field. Those whose talent you can really get excited about. Now start prospecting for them. Start mentioning their talents to those you come in contact with daily. Start doing what you can to send business their way. And when people begin to take your advice and call on that person, you can be sure that in the future the guy you benefited will get around to saying nice things about you. That is, if you warrent them.

WHAT does a politician do to extend his circle of influence? The first thing most men do when they get political aspirations is join up. They join everything the Kiwanis, Rotary, Chamber of Commerce, Elks, Eagles. You know, every fraternal, service, or religious club in town. That's certainly one way to meet people, and some salespeople do most of their business from such contacts. One top producer I know practices magic. For years he's been doing free magic shows for organizations, and in every act I've ever seen him do he's had well planted plugs to let the audience know that his agency sells every type of insurance known to man. And for him that works. He's known to everyone in four countries and does a tremendous business.

JUST yesterday a close friend of mine, a guy that wrote twelve million dollars worth of insurance business last year, told me that he'd felt restless the other day and decided to take a walk up and down Main Street. "I didn't believe it, Art," he told me, "I actually closed three different deals in that one walk. I guess there's a lot more action on the street than in my office some days." When people see you they remember things they've been putting off, so moving around and being seen can be a good practice.

MAKE an honest effort to pick winners for clients. Successful people influence other people's buying. Try to sell to people whom you really respect in their particular profession. You'll soon have dozens of people in other professions you can pitch for. And it'll all come back to you a hundredfold. The lucky circle of influence is like a rolling prairie fire and only you can stop it by failing to give your best to a client.

RELATIVELY speaking, you might be doing great, but unless you become a professional in your attitude and your practice, then all the relatives in the world won't help you. Your lucky circle of influence and it's growth can provide you with unlimited potential for success, and the circles you go around in can mean the difference between growth and disaster.

CHAPTER 17

THE ART OF A SINCERE COMPLIMENT

HOW many compliments do you pay a day? Are you one of those people who carry around a mental checklist? Are you paying out the wrong kind of compliments and wondering why they get such poor results?

HOW many times have you been told that each and every person is an "individual?" Or "everyone is different," "no two alike," "to become a great salesperson you must learn to adapt," "different strokes for different folks?" And if you listen to enough of this "different" advice you soon can become so confused that you prefer to just stay away from people to avoid all that static from making the wrong judgements about what somebody will or will not like.

AS a salesperson or representative, you simply cannot get into that rut of avoiding people. You must get out and mingle if you hope to succeed. And so I'd like to mess up another one of those popular "myths". People really aren't different in at least one aspect. Everyone likes a compliment. And so why is it that some people seem to repel compliments? Why do some people get so uptight when you pay them a compliment? Well, to give you one answer to this question "why", let me tell you about what happened to me just last week. I was in my office and the salesman had called beforehand and made an appointment. I'd set aside an hour and a half to see him and I really had a need for either his product or that of a competitor. And on that particular day I was wearing a really sad sportscoat. I mean it was a wreck. With bulging pockets all pushed out of shape, spotty, and just that morning I'd run into a particularly aggressive used car salesman, and when shaking my hand he'd overdone it and torn some of my sleeve. On my way to the office I'd stopped off at the Salvation Army and tried to give them the sportscoat, but the lady wouldn't accept it. And, so rather than drive to the cleaners and try to retrive one of my other coats that I'd taken that day, I put this rag back on. Now about my tie. I'd also taken that day to take in all of my favorite ties for cleaning, and I was wearing a tie that I had eaten at least my last four lunches on. It was dirty and wrinkled, and to tell you the truth it really wasn't much of a tie when it started out new.

AND would you believe it, that salesman came into my office and after eyeballing me and showing me all of his teeth he had the nerve to say this to me. He said, "That's a nice sportscoat you have on, Art, you have good taste." And then he used that line to tell me that since I had good taste I should certainly see that his product was the best on the market.

A little later he eyeballed me once more and he picked out my tie. "That's an unusual tie you have on, Art, I like it. As you can see, our product is unusual too."

DO you see what he was doing? He was using STOCK COMPLIMENT #1 (Mention the coat), and he was tying his pitch line in with that compliment. Then he went on to STOCK COMPLIMENT #2 (the tie - unusual), and when he finished with the eyeballing and the big teeth showing and the #1 and #2 stock compliments, he'd convinced me that he wasn't to be trusted at all. And as I showed him the door the fellow really didn't know where he'd gone wrong.

WHAT he'd done is insult me. Certainly, everyone likes to receive a compliment. But an honest compliment. And there was nothing more irritating than an undeserved compliment that reveals insincerity. Now that day I just happened to be wearing a new pair of shoes. I picked them up out of town. I paid a small fortune for them. I really was proud of those shoes and they had a shine on them that wouldn't quit. If that fellow had really looked as he did his eyeballing, he'd have spotted the shoes and scored a direct hit with me. He'd a probably made a sale, but when I thought about that beat up sports jacket reflecting my good taste, and how that same good taste should lead me to buy his product, I quivered. When I thought about my miserable tie and how it was unique just like that man's product, I just didn't want that style of uniqueness in my office. And although that salesman thought he was following the rules of smart salesmanship, he was doing what an awful lot of "almost good" salesmen do daily. He was just missing the point. Just missing the target. He was almost attaining greatness by just barely misunderstanding what he should be doing.

HOW are you doing? How are you at compliments? Would you like a guideline so that you might avoid the loss of a sale or a loss of credibility like this salesman did?

THE first rule in paying a compliment is that you must be sincere. I'm sure that if you make your living by using your mouth then you must realize that there is a whole lot more to this communication business than just saying the right words. There is what we sometimes call "body language." The way we look. The gestures we make. The way we move our body. Those dozens of little unconscious things we do that let the listener know if we mean what we are saying. If you've ever sold anything then you know that you must be sold on your product. And that is the way it is with a compliment. In order to sell someone that you are sincere in your praise you must be sincere.

And often it isn't easy to get excited about that tie your prospect is wearing. But if you will only open your eyes, you will see something that catches your eye that you can be sincere with praise about. Look around you when you pay a call on a prospect. If you can see a trophy, a plaque, a photograph, or a painting that bears the name of the prospect, look it over. If it falls into your particular field of interest, if it really means something to you, then comment on it. Look around for something you like. And then honestly say, "Hey, I really like that." And if you can't find anything then avoid complimenting. You can learn to discover a lot of things that warrent compliments once you learn to search. Once you realize that you can't successfully "con" a prospect, you will learn to reach out a bit and seek areas that really win your respect. You might even find yourself doing a bit of research with the gal outside the office while you are waiting to see that prospect.

I got rid of that old tie and that old sports coat and that young salesman all in the same day. And you know something? The very next day a salesman from the fellow's competition called on me and he looked around as he was presenting his sales talk to me. He spotted the pictures of my children and said, "Aren't kids great, Art? I've got two myself and they really keep me hopping. Those kids of yours are just beautiful." And a little later he walked over and touched the plaques I'd won for some article contests. "National Awards", he commented, "that's just great."

WHEN I signed the contract and he was just about to leave, he looked me in the eye and he said, "Mr. Fettig, I've really enjoyed our visit." And you know something, I felt exactly the same way and I told him so.

HOW do the people you work with feel? Can they believe you when you say something nice?

CHAPTER 18

DRINK TO YOUR OWN HEALTH

WHAT is the biggest stumbling block on the road to being lucky? On the road to the top? I mean the top in sales or management or any endeavor. The top in earnings. The top in success. It's booze brothers and sisters, and if you don't believe me, then ask any Sales Manager.

DON'T run away. I do not have a tamberine or the Good Book or membership cards to A.A. for you all to sign. I just want to point out an occupational hazard that faces all salespeople and show you how your drinking habits affect your selling habits and that is what controls the speed in your climb to the top. Isn't it? Your selling habits. A good sales representative will cultivate every good point he can because he realizes that in the final tally every single thing he can get going for him will pay off in sales. Take a look at yourself, The Successful Salesperson. Look at your clothes, your smile, the way you talk, your handshake, your record keeping. Every single thing you do is planned to help you make a sale. Your self-motivation. . .the way you get yourself charged up in the morning to go out and attack the buying world.

NOW back to this drinking idea. Drinking is fine by me. I've got no axe to grind. It is just that I have this allergy and when I take one drink I break out all over with insanity. I have no desire to take up the prohibition cause but I have learned that it is awfully easy to use a drink as a pick me up. As a motivator. A confidence builder. And I've learned something else. Everything a drink gave me is less than what it took away from me in sales efficiency. That old theory - you know it - "for every action there is a reaction." Well with every drink I lost more than I gained.

One thing, a drink is a delay. An excuse from charging right in there and doing the job. A drink is also many times an introduction to another drink. If you don't believe that then some night observe how many people come in for one drink and end up having four or five. Now I don't intend giving you the full business about how alcohol will tear your insides out and send you down the road to ruin. I'm not in the anti-alcohol business. My purpose is to show you how you can increase your income by decreasing your alcoholic intake.

YOU have to take customers or business associates out to drink?. . .maybe it's true. I talked to the top life insurance salesman in town the other evening and he told me about how he used to wine and dine brokers to sell insurance, and after about a year of heavy boozing he suddenly discovered that although it was true that these drinkers trickled in a little business for him, he was making less money trying to sell with booze than in any other manner. In other words, he simply took an inventory and learned that of all of the approaches he was using to sell, boozing was the least productive in income and the most damaging to him physically.

HE has a system now. When a customer makes it evident that he expects the "Drinking Bit," my friend gets him to bring a friend along. He has one drink with them and then makes a point of paying for two more drinks for the customer and his friend. After drinking just one drink he makes an excuse of another appointment and he leaves the scene. He's kept careful score and learned that he makes more sales to the heavy drinker that he treats this way than in any other manner. Contrary to his former opinion, my friend has learned that after you have more than one drink with a client your sales go down in proportion to the number of drinks you stay around for. We tried to dope this out and came up with this theory. After taking the three drinks the customer goes home. If you stay around it gets to four and five drinks and the fellow gets loaded and home late and his wife gives him the devil, he feels rough the next morning and he blames it all on you, the guy who bought the drinks. Crazy? Maybe it is crazy, but when a fellow keeps charts on such things and produces more than a couple of million dollars in sales every year, it is hard to knock his theories.

MEANWHILE my friend actually is out making other calls and making more sales to other clients at the time "the boozer" is having that second and third drink.

MY dear friend, Dottie Walters, President of Hospitality Hostess Service, Author of the Book, "The Selling Power of a Woman," and one of the most dynamic salespeople I know, tells me that she has over 4,000 customers and that she has never taken customer out for a drink. Further, she tells me that she has never known a successful woman in sales who took her customer out to a bar.

I think Dottie is right. For the woman, bars are not conducive to selling. At least not to selling the products and services generally marketed in the sales field.

I don't want to go into the business of the morning after. That is unpleasant enough without talking about it, but lets face it, every salesperson knows he has to get out and get under to make a sale, and if he feels a wreck in the morning after, he has a tough time getting started. The morning after a good night's sleep is a Good Morning, generally, and you certainly know that your sales are better when you feel better.

IT'S the same thing in any occupation. Alcholism causes absenteeism, and when a salesperson is absent from wherever the sales are, they pass him by.

I suppose by now you are expecting me to pass out the pledge cards and the pins for the lapels, but as I said before, your drinking is strictly up to you and I'd be the last guy in the world to try to change it. All I want you to do is sit down and honestly evaluate your drinking. Is it working for you? I mean, is it helping you to be your best? Is it increasing your income? Does your way of drinking keep you in shape? Keep you healthy and eager to do your job? If it doesn't then use your good sale's sense and work at your drinking just like you work at all of the other points that will pay off at the end of the year in net income. Cut out those drinking sales pitches or liquid management meetings if they aren't producing the desired results. Cut out those nights before, if the mornings after are diminishing your productivity.

BUT remember, you don't get a card or a pin or anything else for taking my advice. All you get is higher sales, better results, and greater income, and if that interests you, then Lots of Luck.

CHAPTER 19

"THAT FINISHING QUALITY"

Several years ago a washed up fighter once called Cassius Clay paid a visit to Battle Creek and I had the opportunity to have a private session with him. The owner of the motel where he was staying made the arrangements and Muhammad Ali came into the room with a cocky look about him and that man really revolted me for a while. After all, as a disabled veteran I couldn't think much of his attitude of taking the role of a concientious objector in the Viet Nam struggle where brave American young men were giving their lives. I felt it made sense when they took his boxing crown away from him and I didn't have much sympathy for him or the fact that rumors had it that he was hundreds of thousands of dollars in debt at the time. I shot a number of photographs of him and tried a few personal questions but all I got from him was some double talk and the old "Flit like a butterfly, sting like a bee." I really didn't understand what was going on with that man at all. In the matter of a few moments he grew bored with my approach and left me standing there alone.

Like everyone else, I guess, I followed his career with interest and it wasn't long until I found myself cheering him along with the others.

Maybe what I respected most about the man was that he never lost the faith he had in himself. He hung in there no matter what people said about him. He hung in there tough.

Then a while back Muhammad Ali paid a visit to Milan Federal Prison here in Michigan and a reporter interviewed him and asked him if some of the fights he was having weren't really push overs with no risk involved. He replied, "They're all risks. I'm not that much better than the other fighters. It's just that I have that finish quality." "A race horse wins by a nose, but it still wins. That's the way it is. It's a scary feeling to be in the late rounds. You're tired and you're sore and your corner tells you its still even. That's when you have to have the "finish quality" and I've been blessed by God to be given the will to do it."

I run an audio-visual shop and when you are producing an audio-visual show you really have nothing at all until you have that last slide in the tray and the final work done on your sound track. Until you have everything you have nothing. And we have a couple of young men that work for me on a part time basis. I have found that it is fun to take young people with great talent and train them and challenge them and maybe teach them a little about living as well as working. And so often I find that they fall into the trap of telling me why they didn't accomplish something. For instance, one came in and told me that he didn't get a show shipped as requested because there was no wrapping paper. I handed him a sack and we wrapped it in that. Another time I was told that they couldn't ship a show because they didn't know the man's address. It was in the in-house phone book on the desk. Now Dennis Jenkins is a fine artist and Dan Strowbridge is developing into a top-notch photographer and it is exciting to watch their talents develop with each new challenge that I give them. . . .but, it is even more exciting as I watch them develop their finishing ability.

We put up a new sign in our office. Our office is loaded with signs but we made this one bigger than the others and gave it a more prominent spot. It reads. . ."Don't tell me why you couldn't, tell me how you did."

In other words, I don't want to know what obstacles stopped you, I want to know how you overcame them in order to report that you succeeded.

Isn't that music to your ears too? "We did it. We finished. It's done."

DON'T TELL ME WHY YOU

COULDN'T. . . . . . .

TELL ME HOW YOU DID!

CHAPTER 20

"USE LUCKY WORDS"

WORDS are the tools of anyone engaged in this exciting business of selling. What you are says a whole lot about you and we are discovering more and more that in this business of communications that the actual words do not communicate nearly as much as the tone and manner in which we use words. Timing means a great deal, body language often reveals much more than we wish it would and I'm beginning to believe that the gut feeling we produce in others is more important than anything else we do in the business of communication. Learning to produce the right gut feeling just might some day be the only course taught in selling. But today, right now words are still important. And for a few minutes I want to examine words.

A Yale Professor did a lot of research recently on words, and he singled out the 17 most persuasive words in the English language. We call them lucky words. These are not listed necessarily in their order of importance. . .I would guess that the law of different strokes for different folks applies to what would be considered "the" most persuasive word. Here they are and I hope you'll give them some thought as you read them over:

YOU

SAVE

NEW

RESULTS

MONEY

HEALTH

EASY

SAFETY

LOVE

DISCOVERY

PROVEN

GUARANTEE

ADVANTAGE
POSITIVE
BENEFITS
NOW
SECURITY

Now that you have read the words, I'd like you to conduct your own little experiment. Take the words and the next time that you want to buy something try to see what it was that caused that desire to buy. If you read an ad in the paper and de-

cide to buy, check the words in the ad with this list of words. If you hear something on the radio or on TV and decide that you want something, check the words used. Look at the advertising that you read. And. . . .next time you are writing a letter see if you can't use those words of persuasion more effectively. Next time you make a sales presentation look at your language. Can you put these words to work for you? These words are proven. Guaranteed. They will help you, save you time, get you the benefits and results now. Check those last few sentences you've just read. See what I mean? Now try words of persuasion in your next communication. Lucky words.

CHAPTER 21

"TURN ON YOUR LIVING"

EVER meet a guy or a gal who seemed excited and turned on about everything? Who seemed to get a kick out of just eating an apple, a prune, an orange, or maybe just a handful of nuts? As they race along the streets they showed you things you never noticed before, statues, unusual buildings, maybe a squirrel or a robin or a beautiful sunset. They were in a bit of a hurry, no time to waste on idle gossip, and yet there was a fullness in their activity. They wore a smile as wide as the Pacific and had a happy word and observation for every human being they met. Maybe they talked to dogs, too, and birds and squirrels, and they seemed to notice and talk back. Somehow they sensed it when you wore a new hat or when the lady down the block had a new coat. They passed out compliments like they had an extra basketfull and you just knew for sure that these words came straight from their heart.

DON'T you wish you had the luck to be as interesting and happy as they were? You can, you know. It might take a lot of getting out of the rut you are in; you have to practice new things. It's clumsy at first. It isn't easy to wear a smile in the early morning if you aren't used to it. It feels strange on your mouth when you turn the corners up and show your teeth, but if you try it then your mouth gets used to the idea and pretty soon you are smiling a big friendly smile and it doesn't hurt a bit. Noticing the world around you takes a bit of doing. We get into such habits of living that everything is automatic. We feed the necessary data for survival into our subconscious minds and then run on automatic pilot from then on. That's where dull living comes from, running automatic. Nothing really happens, life just goes on. We eat, we sleep, we work, and we die, and we hardly realize that any of this is taking place.

THOSE who are having such fun with their lives refuse to go automatic. They use their senses to make life alive. They smell things, taste their food, touch people with their hands by shaking hands with them, patting them on the back. They look and drink in life's beauty at every opportunity. They observe

people, what they are wearing, their happiness and sorrow. They know how to pass out sincere compliments because they observe those things that rate complimenting.

FOR several unhappy years I ran completely on automatic pilot. I was a real dud. Somehow I concluded that I was magnificent and above those around me. I withdrew and simply existed. Life became a real drag. No adventure. No excitement. No anticipation. No joy. Then I encountered a few self improvement books and I tried a few of the things they suggested. I made an honest effort to do something good for my fellow man every single day. I plotted, I planned, I worked at it with a passion and it became a good habit. Next, I began to observe the people I met. Some people get so much more out of life than others. Some get so very little joy. I observed that the pill poppers and heavy drinkers were generally unhappy. Same with heavy smokers. Now, you do your own thing. You are you and I am me, and I wouldn't have it any other way. I simply observed this and so I quit drinking, quit smoking and I suddenly liked the people around me a whole lot more. I started expanding my senses. My taste buds came alive. Eating a fresh, juicy orange became a real event. I began shaking hands, looking at people, listening to them, their troubles, and as I did I noticed that their troubles seemed to ease up, once they talked about them. I started caring, really caring, about the people I met. Right about then they started caring about me.

IF you meet a guy who is really excited about life it just might be me. Thank God, yes, it just might be me. I'm that guy with the perfectly normal feeling on my face when my smile is as wide as the Pacific. No more survival programing for me now. I'm turned on for good. Life is now everything those old fashioned happy songs said it was, and you'll agree if you just try this intensive living scheme.

1. Smile. Every morning, at everyone you meet. Sure, it will seem unnatural and odd at first, but work on it daily. You'll soon feel as happy as you look, and when that time comes it will no longer be unnatural.

2. Shake hands. Touch people in a polite, friendly way. Put warmth into your greetings and your goodbyes.

3. Open your eyes. Make yourself see something new every day. Look at nature whenever you find it. Trees, lakes, animals. Get to a park and feel the grass, it'll expand your sense of living.

4. Pay a compliment to everyone you meet, provided that you can find one thing about that person you sincerely like. If you can't find something then look again. My son told a fat girl at a dance, "You sweat less than any fat girl I ever danced with."

5. Put new life into your walk. Pretend you are a ballerina and your guy just proposed. Skip a little if you dare, and while you are at it give a little whistle. Happiness is a state of mind and you can actually increase your happiness by acting happy.

6. Think about what you think about when you dream. Make a few goals and set out to become the person you wish you were.

7. Try to listen to other people. Just force yourself to listen so hard that you really understand what they are trying to communicate. Watch their faces. Just listening can do more for others than you believe possible. When there is a lull in the conversation, don't feel obligated to fill in right away. Give the other party an opportunity to collect their thoughts and express their opinions. Look at people and smile, and listen.

8. Try new foods. Make eating an adventure. Go out of your way to go out of your way in eating. Save up and invite someone new to lunch. It will be a new experience for both of you.

9. Don't let the world's problems get you down. Remember the prayer, "God grant me the serenity to accept the things I cannot change, the courage to change the things I can, and the wisdom to know the difference."

10. Reach out! Get to know others. Don't raise a wall of indifference. Get involved with others and you'll find that your life takes on a whole new dimension.

THE next time you notice people who seem happy and turned on about everything, observe them closely. What tricks for happy living have they learned that you can add to the above list? Study the happy people in the world and you'll learn that they are all active, involved people. Someone told me, "Happiness is having something pending." I'd change that to "Happiness is involvement."

TRY it and see if I'm right.

CHAPTER 22

HAVE A LUCKY SMILE

SMILE, you're on Candid Camera. Is that a reason to smile? Because thousands of people you don't even know might be watching you? Ridiculous. Smile, yes, but not just because you are on TV. You are on live and in living color to everyone you see every day and smiling is one of the luckiest things you can do.

IN New York City a successful insurance company spends a considerable amount of money every year teaching its salesmen how to smile. They hire a very fine and well known theatrical instructor and he spends hours with each man teaching him how to smile honestly. It pays off, though, every student increases his sales substantially once he learns to smile.

WATCH those beauty queens. The ones who make the finals. For a change, watch them smile. They can smile for hours at a time and still make that smile look real and sincere.

WEBSTER says this about a smile; "To show pleasure, amusement, affection, irony, etc., by an upward curving of the mouth and a sparkling of the eyes." Now I'm not one to differ with Webster, but I think that a smile is more than just a sign. I think it is a flashing tip-off as to what kind of a person you are. If you smile then you are using an outward sign to show an inward glow. A smile is the inner joy in you breaking out.

I just read that dentists have the second highest suicide rate of any group of professionals. Psychologists were first. There were a number of reasons listed. One is that dentists are perfectionalists in a job where perfection is generally impossible. That they worked under a great deal of stress and people often considered them outsiders to the human race because they associated them with a painful experience.

I'd like to take a second to pay tribute to my dentist, Dr. Jerry C. Borsum, D.D.S. of Battle Creek, Michigan. Jerry changed my smile. You see, mine used to always have my hand in front of it because I had this one front tooth that had a hole worn away and it really bothered me. It took Jerry over a year but he finally persuaded me that I needed a complete overhaul job on my mouth and. . .well. . .it cost me a lot but there is one thing that I've got, its my smile. And believe me it made a big difference in my whole attitude towards myself. Thanks Jerry.

DON'T think that you have to have the finest, straightest set of teeth to have an attractive smile either. Sure, you should keep your teeth in shape and keep them as attractive as you can, but smiling is not just a show of teeth. It's a show of joy, and people look at the smile and what it means, not the teeth you show.

LAST week I went out on a call with one of the most successful salesmen I know. He smiles a lot. He smiles as he delivers his sales message, and I noticed that the customer was smiling right back at him. Smiles are like that. Contagious. Like a yawn too. Watch someone smile with a smile that you feel is sincere and sure enough soon you'll catch yourself smiling too.

SOMETHING else I've discovered. If you force yourself to smile when you don't have that inner happiness you'll soon get that inner happiness to go with the look. You start thinking happy thoughts and pretty soon the whole world around you seems like a better place.

SMILING isn't necessarily an ambitious person's game either. It is a well known fact that it takes a lot fewer muscles to smile than to frown. If you are just naturally lazy, then follow your impulse, wear the expression that is the least wearing. Wear a smile. If you want a better, more successful life, then wear a smile.

WHEN tragedy strikes you can cry but after that cry get up and live again. Live life full force, and living, really living, calls for a great deal of smiling. Smiling is enjoying and what kind of a life are you living if it doesn't involve a great deal of enjoying? Mighty dull. Counting one's blessings brings on a great deal of sincere smiling. Don't go looking around you at all of the things you don't have. Look at what you have and enjoy it. Smile over it and appreciate your good health.

YES, smile though your heart is breaking. You've heard those words in that song. "You'll find that life can be worthwhile, if you'll just smile." Try it, wear a lucky smile.

CHAPTER 23

THINK PLUS - IT ADDS UP TO SUCCESS

DO you know this formula? Positive thoughts plus positive actions equal positive results. It is a simple formula for success. Follow it and you will succeed. Ignore it and you will fail. Positive thinking produces greater luck.

YEARS ago, my son brought home the results of an experiment in positive thinking. Success thinking. Can-do thinking. Daniel was in the 5th grade and at school they graded him in 12 different subjects. A few months before he'd brought us seven failing marks. It floored me. I was dumbfounded. I talked to him and to his teacher and I discovered that Daniel believed he was dumb. Stupid. Unable to do the work. He felt that he was a failure. I did a little more checking and reviewing of his marks and realized that his handwriting was so poor that even when he knew the correct answer you couldn't read it. His reading was so poor that he couldn't read the question correctly and his spelling was so bad that if he read the question correctly he misspelled his answer in such poor handwriting that even a correct answer had little chance of getting marked correctly.

THAT evening I sat down with Daniel and had him write this sentence on a piece of paper. "By my next marking I will have at least all passing grades." I told him to write it and believe it. I asked Daniel how he felt bringing home such a miserable card and he admitted that he felt terrible coming home with such a card. I looked him dead in the eye and said, "Daniel, you will never have to have that bad feeling again in your life. From now on you bring home passing grades."

I must admit I brainwashed that kid. Every morning I made him repeat that thought. "By my next marking I will have at least all passing grades." We did a little work on his reading and writing and spelling. I explained to him that learning was like building a brick wall. If you failed to learn something properly in the lower grades it was like putting marshmallows in your wall instead of bricks, and as you went to build your wall higher the whole thing would collapse. I told him that he had a few marshmallows and we'd have to replace them with good bricks.

WE worked a few minutes each evening, and I must admit that after a couple of weeks I let him skip his extra work but I stuck right to the "believing" business. Every day Daniel went to school believing he would get passing grades.

THEN one evening Daniel brought home his report card, and with the exception of a C minus in handwriting, every mark was average or above. He even had a B in arithmetic. When I first had Daniel write down that goal I thought it was impossible. Daniel thought it was impossible, but I told him he had to believe it. I told myself I had to believe in him and sure enough, he came through.

FOR a while, my daughter, Nancy, was a poor math student. Nancy is a bright girl. Lots of A's and B's, and she has a bright mind. I spent less than 15 minutes telling her what a bright girl she was. That she was good at math. I made her write down this sentence. "From now on I am good at math." A few moments later I actually noted the improvement. Her whole attitude changed. A short time later she asked me to check her homework, and when I did it was perfect. She wanted to do some extra work just to make certain she understood some of the things that bothered her so much a few months before, and she went through the problems in a breeze. I can't measure the improvement in simple percentages, but believe me, the difference was like the difference of night and day, light and dark, right and wrong.

WE used to drive one of Nancy's friends to school each morning. One day she came to our house all tensed up about an achievement test she had that day. The day before she had taken part of the test and tensed up so badly that her mind went blank. She told me how important the test was and she knew she'd tense up again. I told her to write this sentence on a piece of paper. "I will do well in that test today without worry or tension." What bothered her was the number of answers she had to mark I DON'T KNOW. I explained to her that an achievement test was like a man checking the level of a coal bin. He wanted to see how full it was. The test was to see how full her mind was, and if she was smart enough to really know what she knew and what she didn't know then she was really learning. I told her that if the test showed she had a full bin, knew all the answers, then there would be no need for her to go to school any longer.

WELL, she wrote the sentence as I asked and the next day she told me how easy the test had been. She was the first one done.

Knew most of the answers and didn't have the least bit of trouble. She thinks I have a magic formula, and I think so too.

SOME time ago, our church undertook a building program. We needed roughly $200,000, and wisely our Pastor called in a professional group to undertake the money raising campaign. I went to the first meeting with a big minus sign in my mind. I couldn't believe it was possible to raise such a sum. Yet, when I left that first meeting I was convinced that we would make that goal with ease. I shouldn't say with ease, because we were let in on the secret that it would involve hard work and persistence, but those professional collectors completely convinced us with their positive attitude that this goal would easily be reached. Well, to make a long, hard effort short and sweet, we went over the goal in eight weeks. None of us was surprised when we went over the top, because after that first meeting we believed it would happen, and believing and taking positive action made it happen.

IN recent months this Power of Plus Thinking has shown positive results in so many ways. When you learn the secret of Plus, then the people you meet and talk to, shout out how they are doing, how they are going to do. Failures and future failures tip off their hands with sentences like, "I don't think I'll get that promotion but. . ." or "I guess this is a waste of time but. . ."

WE have a nice job opening in our company. It will mean a big raise in salary for the successful candidate, and of the three or four people eligible, one is remarkable unqualified. His education, past performance, reputation, are all against him. He believes he will get that promotion and he is acting in a purely positive manner. The other candidates are running around thinking negative minus thoughts. It is interesting to watch a thing like this, and yet in my own mind I already know who that promotion will go to. To the person with the positive attitude about the job. He's showing those around him that he feels qualified. He had things going for him just because of the way he acts, looks and talks. He looks confident. I truly believe he will completely outclass the other people, even though he is the least qualified. It's hard to stop a person with all plus signs.

LISTEN to what people around you say. "I don't have time to read that Success Magazine." Give them a big minus score on that one. "I don't think he'll buy this but. . .". "I don't suppose you'd want to buy one of these. . .".

NOW look at the outstanding successes that you know. Notice the PLUS SIGN shining in their eyes. ALL PLUS SIGNS. "I can't afford not to read Success Magazine." "He's going to buy this from me." "I'm sure you'll want to have one of these."

FROM the time you first learn to hold a rattle you are dealing with plus and minus. Success and failure are the total score you compile in a lifetime and that score will depend solely on your own attitude.

IF you don't believe it, then try a little experiment. Write something down on a piece of paper. Something positive. Now believe it. . .Work on it and watch the impossible happen. Watch your luck change for the better.

THE way you think, the way you believe is what you are. Think success and you'll achieve it.

CHAPTER 24

ASPIRING

HOW good are you at selling? At selling a product, or at selling yourself or at selling your ideas? About 90% of all of the ideas in the world never see the dawn of application. No. . .I suppose it would be closer to 99% or possibly 99.9%. Most ideas die in the initial stages. And most people fail miserably at selling themselves. Even successful people function at only a small percentage of their real potential.

MIKE Vance, former Executive Director for Walt Disney, once remarked that he believed that hell would be a place where a man must see clearly just what he might have been in life, and was not. . .for a man to see his real potential.

PROFESSIONAL salesmen have many different courses available to them for the sole purpose of making them succeed at just one thing. . .Selling. And closing the sale is what selling is all about. Getting the signature on the dotted line. And in this business of communication many many times we are really endeavoring to sell ourselves or an idea. The major reason that most people fail is that they fail to discover closing techniques that work. Let us examine the techniques that sales people use and see if we can find an application of these techniques to our own quest for better communication.

ONE of the best models for successful closing is a system I call the "Aspiring Technique." The word "aspire" comes from the Latin aspirare. . .meaning "breathe to." I like to believe that the aspiring technique will put life and breath to your project or goal. The word is defined as follows: To breath on, in, or forth; pant or long for; attempt; attain; to long, aim, or seek ambitiously. And we take the letters of the word A-S-P-I-R-I-N-G as the keys to selling and getting approval for what we seek.

A ASSUMPTIVE ATTITUDE

S SUBORDINATE QUESTION

P PHYSICAL ACTION

I IMPENDING EVENT

R RELATED STORY

I INVITE

N NOW

G GET

THE letter A stands for the Assumptive Attitude. For me, the assumptive close is the most successful. It simply means that you assume that the other guy will buy you, or your idea, or the product you are selling, and you act on that assumption. If you really believe in what you are selling it is very easy for you to assume that you will succeed. You simply take the attitude that you will get a positive result. You proceed with what must be done. If it calls for a signature on the contract, you fill in the information required on the contract, and as you do so you continue to talk up your product or idea. You repeat the good things that your prospect will enjoy because of this transaction. If the prospect doesn't stop you, you go right ahead and then offer the completed contract for signature. Some call this the "Don't Stop Me Close." Others call it the "Order Blank Close." No matter what you call it, it often does the job. The opposite of this technique is what too many people use daily without being aware of their style. They walk in and say, "You don't want any of these do you?" Then they wonder why they fail.

OUR second style of close for the letter S is called the "Subordinate Question." Here we ask for a minor decision. It's just a little decision that is easy to make. However, the minor decision usually carries with it a major decision. "Charlie, I'm your representative for the United Way, and based on your annual salary the recommended donation for your family is $500. Would it be easier to pay this at $50 a month or would you prefer to take care of it all at once?" It Charlie replies that he could only handle it on a $50 a month basis, he has made only a minor decision, but in reality he has also agreed to the $500 fair share of the figure. "Do you want me to start this Friday and Monday?" "Should I order fifty or a hundred?" "Should I call Sam right now and tell him you approved this or will you?" For good reason, this is also referred to as "The Multiple Choice Of Yes Technique."

"P" stands for Physical Action. While I've had a few successes with people when they were shaking their head "no," I've had a whole lot more when they were nodding "yes." Just the act of nodding is a physical action. I often try to preface a close with some questions that I know we agree upon. And I get a bit more physical myself at this point. Upon agreement of a point I might nod and wink and I notice that the other fellow replies with a nod and wink. But then occasionally when I offer the pen and the contract he seems to freeze. Nothing happens. Some salesmen call this "presale paralysis." It is dangerous to just let the fellow sit there frozen. When I see this happen, I move. Maybe I just stand up. That action alone will sometimes start him writing. If he remains frozen then I take the contract and say, "Let me check that, I want to make sure it is correct." I look it over carefully, smile, hand it back and say, "Yep, it's right. Just put your John Hancock right here Charlie," or "just write your name here."

ONCE when trying to get a signature after hours of negotiations, I simply threw the contract in the wastebasket and pointed to the door. The fellow was completely shaken, he went straight to the basket, took out the contract and signed it. Then he picked it up and handed it to me with a look that said, "Now try and get out of that one."

PHYSICAL action. All it does is take the other person's mind off a logjam and get it rolling again. . .your way. One warning . . .don't overdo it. Do it gradually. Too much action can shake a guy up. You might completely divert his train of thought.

IMPENDING event is our next close. Any event that might happen in the near future that would affect the transaction. A proposed price increase. A heavy work schedule that would make the project impossible next month. Something that would diminish the benefits that could be obtained through immediate action. Getting in on the ground floor before the best locations are taken.

THIS close is based on fear of loss, fear of looking bad. . .fear of being outclassed by competition. Personally, the impending event close is my greatest weakness. How many ads draw you to to a store when they read, "Sunday and Monday Only," "Limited Supply," "First Hundred Customers Only?" The impending event is that either time or supply will run out. An expected price rise often gets me moving off dead center.

"R" stands for Related Story. In selling, speaking, writing. . . yes, in producing audio visual shows too, the related story is one of the best tools for getting a point across. For some reason, when I am billed to speak to an audience I usually draw a larger crowd than the previous speaker. I really don't know the exact reason why this happens. My name isn't well known. My picture isn't that appealing. I would guess that the combination of Humor, Motivation and Creativity has a certain appeal of its own that somehow works. Anyway, when I quote my fee, a lot of program chairmen get a little shaky. I say this, "Joe Benning at X Chamber of Commerce was a bit worried about my fee, too, but we went ahead and hired me. With the larger audience we drew, he actually came out ahead." It is a true story. He could call Joe and it would be confirmed. Ninety five percent of the people in the world do what other people do. Only 5% are innovative and, therefore, stories about what other people have done, especially what important, successful, influential people have done in this regard are important to your prospect. That is why I often tell a prospect what other firms have done with me in this or that regard. It makes them feel that a similar decision by them would be a right decision. People love "for instances" when they apply directly to the subject at hand.

THE second "I" in aspiring stands for Invite. Invite the prospect to buy. To buy you, to buy your idea, to buy your product. Ask for agreement. "Will you go along with me on this, George?" "May I send this order in today?" "Am I hired?" "Shall we put this program in effect today?" An awful lot of amateur communicators go through all of the motions of making a presentation and then get chickenhearted. They actually change the subject and leave without ever asking for the sale. And when they do this they really let the other person down. They leave the burden of concluding up to the other guy. Too often a successful outcome isn't lost, it is thrown away. Invite. Ask. Come right out and request a positive decision. If you feel that you would rather not ask then. . .welcome to the club. Everyone has that feeling because this business of asking involves the risk of being rejected. What you must realize is this. . .If you fail to ask then you probably will fail. And when your idea or your product doesn't sell it isn't you personally that is being rejected. Invite your prospect to buy and you will often succeed.

THE Letter "N" in aspiring is for NOW. Not tomorrow. Not next year. NOW. "I assume you will want to get started on this project right NOW. Is that right?" "Don't you agree that there is no better time to start this than right this moment?" "Before our stock runs low I'm sure you want this mailed in NOW." Urgency is often an essential ingredient. Most projects that are temporarily set aside remain set aside forever. "Let's do it now," should be included in every thing you attempt.

"G". The final letter in aspiring reminds us to GET. Get the order. Get the agreement. Get what you wanted to get and then just GET. Get out. Get going to another prospect. Just

GET. Don't stick around and chat once the deal is made. Too many times salespeople buy the sale back just because they don't have the good sense to quit when they are winners.

A S P I R I N G. Whether you are aspiring to sell a product, a service, an idea, or whether you are just making a real attempt to communicate an idea. . .remember the Aspiring Technique. It will breathe the elements of luck into your endeavor.

CHAPTER 25

LISTEN

WANT to know the best word of advice I've ever heard? "Listen." That's it, just "Listen."

ONE of the most difficult lessons in the world for a human to learn is that he doesn't learn much when he's talking. Oh, he might discover how little he knows about the subject he's discussing, but usually he learns absolutely nothing.

I'M a talker. I guess you might say that I've got one of the biggest mouths in this section of the country, and with all the politicians hereabouts, that's saying something. Somehow, over the past few years I've developed this eerie sense of responsibility that compels me to wipe out silence whenever and wherever I encounter it. I'm sort of a lull liquidator. Even a "Quiet Hospital Zone" sign seems like a personal insult to me.

NOW liquidating lulls isn't a major crime in itself, but once you get into the habit, you often get out-of-hand. Often you might believe that a lull exists, when in reality, the other guy is just trying to catch his breath. Probably he's worn out from the battle of getting a word in edgewise.

NOW about that idea that "Listen" is such a great piece of advice. Recently I had the rare honor of attending a Sensitivity Training Program. Maybe you've heard about them. It's a sort of "Getting to know yourself better session." Contrary to what you might have heard through the grapevine, Sensitivity Training isn't mass ego suicide. It isn't nudity and games either. At least not the session I attended. We didn't get to know each other that well or that way. More than anything, we got to know ourselves, and like a crane collapsing on my skull, I got one message loud and clear. I'm a lull liquidator and it gets obnoxious to everyone, especially the liquidator himself, once he becomes aware of his problem.

I think the first hint I got of my problem was when one of our members smiled at me gently and said, "SHUT UP, ART. JUST SHUT UP!"

SHUT-UP
ART.!!

I was a little shocked at this but when half a dozen other voices joined in and said, "YEAH, WILL YOU SHUT UP, ART," I began to realize that not every one of them was sitting on the edge of the chair waiting for my next words of wisdom. I shut up. First I sulked. Two sessions I sulked and then someone unjustly accused me of sulking. At least I felt it was unjust. "I wasn't sulking," I argued, "I was thinking."

AND then when they asked what words of wisdom I had come up with in one and a half sessions of thinking, all I could reply was, "I was thinking how amazing it is that you people have been able to handle the lulls without me."

AND after we all laughed I started listening, and from then on life took on a new meaning for me. Learning to listen was one of my luckiest lessons.

I was like Mark Twain when he became middle aged and was amazed at all his father had learned since Mark was a teenager. I was amazed at how interesting and intelligent that gang was, and since I started listening I've discovered how really interesting people are.

ARE you a lull liquidator? You can find out easy enough. Take a look at your conversations with others. How much listening do you do? Next time there is a pause in the conversation, just wait. Wait for that other guy to start something. That is where new areas of thought come from. You just might suddenly discover that you've been steering conversations and in that way you have greatly impeded your intake of new ideas and different knowledge. Letting the other person take the lead can give you a great deal of insight into what is really important to your friends and acquaintances.

IT isn't easy to convert. At first, those lulls seem almost embarrasing, but once you learn to count ten before you talk again, you find that someone is always willing to take up the conversation.

OF course, there are ways to encourage others to open up with their interests. Many successful salespeople have learned to carefully scrutinize their prospect's desk and the walls of the office for hints on what interests the client. Trophies, unusual paper weights, pictures of the family, or maybe a huge swordfish hanging on the wall. A sharp salesperson uses these subjects to loosen a prospect up before making his presentation. Even a tie-pin can be revealing.

RECENTLY, I attended the funeral of a fellow worker. I listened quietly as the man delivering the eulogy recounted some of the activities my friend had participated in. Overhauling and maintaining the church's buses, substitute driver, usher. And on and on the list went, and to me that man was a totally different man than the one I knew. The man I knew never said much about himself. Never talked about his private life. He was more of a listener, I decided. And was he? Or was he just a little slow on the trigger? Too slow to even fire a word in edgewise? Maybe I never gave him a lull to work with. I wonder how many thousands of others I've shortchanged that way?

OF course, it would be unreasonable to go the other route. The route of a silent sulker. Conversation is an art and it is truly a joint effort. A meeting of the minds. Both minds. Sure, contribute. Say your say and say it well. But say it once and then allow a little silence so that the other person can say his piece.

I still liquidate lulls. Real lulls. But they have to be humdingers, not just pauses. I count to ten now, and if the lull is still there I pounce on it with gusto. And oh, how things have changed. There's a whole new world out there I was missing. A world full of interesting people and to think I discovered that world just because someone cared enough, had the sense and sensitivity to cry out loud and clear, "SHUT UP ART, JUST SHUT UP." I did, and I discovered that listening is really fun. Listening can be your luckiest skill!

CHAPTER 26

"DO UNTO OTHERS"

ONE of the greatest secrets of business success is this "treat your customers as you yourself would like to be treated." Now, isn't that enlightening? Exciting? Startling? No. It is as old as mankind. An application of the Golden Rule. You'll find it in the Bible if you happen to be a Christian. It's contained in Matthew 7:12. "Whatsoever you will that men would do to you, do so to them; for this is the law of the prophets."

I'VE heard some fast dealers rephrase this. "Do it to them before they do it to you." They think they are outsmarting their fellow man, but since they reap what they sow they are actually outsmarting themselves.

WHAT is so amazing about this Golden Rule is that every major religion came up with the same yardstick for us in measuring our relationship with our fellow man.

THE Buddist's have it in Udanvarga 5:18. "Hurt not others in ways that you yourself would find hurtful."

HINDUISM says it this way in Mahabharata 5:1517. "This is the sum of duty; do naught unto others which would cause you pain if done to you."

THE Islam's Sunan says, "No one of you is a believer until he desires for his brother that which he desires for himself."

THE Jewish faith finds it in Talmud, Shatbat 31a, "What is hateful to you, do not to your fellow man. That is the entire Law: all the rest is commentary."

WHAT is truly astounding is that this Golden Rule is broken daily by a world full of unhappy people who simply cannot understand why they cannot find happiness. Happiness is in giving and sharing and loving. Happiness is in stretching the Golden Rule the other guy's way instead of your own. As we tilt the scales of justice our way, we love ourselves a little less and in so doing we give up a certain amount of serenity, pride, integrity.

TAKE the headlines of today's newspaper and apply the

Golden Rule to the facts. Whatever is troubling our Nation or the World is made a little worse because men insist on bending the Golden Rule. Greed, Lust, Deceit, Racial inequality and injustice. War. Hatred. Yes, even labor trouble stems from people's inability to follow the rules of their religious belief, no matter what their religious belief might be. Unless a person worships the almighty dollar, I cannot understand how he can daily assault the Golden Rule and then honestly wonder why happiness and satisfaction eludes him.

WANT to become a happier person? Want to feel as if someone removed a heavy yoke from your neck? Want to rid yourself of acid indigestion without a pack of pills? Then get out your Golden Ruler and put it to work for you. Use it daily when you deal with everyone you meet. Sell yes, but use tact, and tell the truth, even if it hurts a little. Introduce the element of honesty into your business dealings. People are basically honest. If they appear dishonest then it is possible that they are simply reacting to you. When people don't trust you they overguard and this very overguarding appears to be dishonesty. Lay down your arms, stick your chin out in a spirit of true honesty. Mention the Golden Rule in your conversation and then follow it. At first everyone might be a little amazed but in time you'll see signs that others are dusting off their Golden Rules too.

BE a pioneer in the field of honesty. We have a tremendous task. Maybe we could get those people in television to let a little of that hot air out of their commercials. Nobody really believes those lies and exaggerations anyway, so why not get down to the real truth about products being advertised? Let's get honest in our conversation. Sure, compliment the other person, but take the time to find something that actually deserves complimenting. Often being tactful is wiser than being "Frank." You'll be amazed at how little you know or observe in the people you see every day.

AS you put honesty and truthfulness into your life you'll find your image of yourself improving. You'll stand a little taller (that yoke is gone). Happiness will become your daily ally, something that goes with you and your frequent smile.

MONEY? Isn't it expensive in this day and age to be really honest? I don't think so. If you are gaining riches through dishonestly, then I cannot believe that you can enjoy the things your money buys. I simply cannot believe that a truly dishonest

GOLDEN
RULE

person can be truly happy. Try the honest way anyway, and see if your money income doesn't actually increase. And the things your money will buy will bring you smiles and happiness because I just must believe that you'll be spending a little less on yourself and a little more on your fellowman, and that's what happiness really is. Giving your fellow man something that you hope someone will give you some day. True luck and true happiness comes in the giving and not in the receiving, and when the world reads the words of the wise men through the ages, they'll find that the secret to a full life can be found in just a few words. "Do unto others as you would have them do unto you."

CHAPTER 27

"GOALS"

HOW many people, do you think, ever sat down and set themselves a goal like this, "I think I'll become a two pack a day cigarette smoker?" Who ever decided, "Guess I'll become a speed freak?" And of the millions of alcoholics in this nation, how many do you believe planned it this way, "In the next twelve months I will become addicted to ethyl alcohol?"

NO. It doesn't happen like that. People experiment with cigarettes and soon discover that they can't do without them. Others just take one marijuana cigarette to see what it's like and they soon progress to "speed" or "hash" or maybe heroin, and then they are hooked. And nearly all alcoholics will tell you that they started out just being "social" and ended up about as unsocial as you can get.

IN other words, people who become victims of alcohol and nicotine and narcotics do so without the slightest bit of planning. That is why these uncontrollable habits are so difficult to understand by people who are not addicts. How many times have you heard it said, "If he were a man he'd just quit?" Or, "Why can't she act like a lady?"

AND so if so many people fall into these damaging habits without any pre-planning, isn't that a warning that if you want to avoid these pitfalls then you must do a little planning beforehand?

LOOK around you. At the outstanding successes in this world. How many of them just fell into success? How many of them just lucked out? Maybe an isolated one or two, but nearly everyone who is successful is successful because of hard work and careful future planning. Good results are brought about by setting goals and working towards them. That's why a person should do a lot of pre-thinking before he starts experimenting with nicotine, alcohol, or narcotics. He should sit down and face the hard facts about what happens to others and he must be willing to pay that same costly price himself if he wants to gamble. Some of the most costly journeys in the world are started on the slightest whim. "Let me try one of those. What do they taste like, anyway?" "I guess one won't hurt." "Well, it is a special occasion and I don't want to be a party pooper."

ON the night I graduated from high school, several graduates had convinced their parents that they were now mature enough to have a little beer and whiskey at their graduation parties. Some young people were drinking alcohol for the first time. One young man, an honor student with a bright future ahead, attended four different parties, and at each he had just one drink, to be one of the boys. Later in the evening he was involved in an auto accident while driving under the influence of alcohol, and he died that same night in the hospital. You might say that he drank himself to death in just one evening.

GOALS. That young man had a list of goals for his future. He was enrolled in a fine university. He had a scholarship he'd worked hard to win. He'd already planned to become a doctor and everything was fitting into place for him and his future. But when he tried that first drink he didn't take the time to fit it into his planning. He didn't take the time to think about how that fitted into his future, and because of that his future ended that very evening.

SMOKING and drinking and taking narcotics call for a great deal of planning and thinking. Think about your life. Think about your future. Think about what you want and what you hope for and then think about the cost you must pay for one of these habits.

ONE reformed alcoholic told me, "I had my whole life planned out. I had a good education, a wonderful family, a fine job. Everything was just great, and for some stupid reason I thought that a few drinks in the evening would make it all even better. Well, those evening drinks soon became morning drinks too, and now I've lost everything. I'm broke, divorced, unemployed and my liver is a mess. I'm a wreck and now that I'm dried out I'm planning to start all over again. I'm setting goals and believe me, there is no place in my planning for alcohol. I've learned that alcohol can mess up the best laid plans. Oh, I'm planning about alcohol though. I'm planning to stay away from it permanently."

TAKE a look at a heavy smoker. Watch him. Notice how his system demands more nicotine every half hour or so. It's a drain on his health and on his pocketbook. Do you want to pay this price? Look at that alcoholic on Skid Row and consider the price he is paying. And look at that narcotic addict. You can visit your local jail and find a victim of narcotics. That prisoner who was just arrested for breaking and entering or robbery or possibly prostitution was probably motivated by the high cost of a drug habit.

PLAN for your future, and while you are planning think about how habits can play a part in your failure or your success. How does smoking fit into your planning? Is there a place for a narcotic habit? And can you pay the price that alcohol demands of its victims?

A fellow worker paid into our pension plan for nearly thirty-eight years and when he retired he was a sick man suffering from emphysema, a disease caused by heavy smoking. He'd planned to have a long, happy retirement and he'd dreamed of all of the wonderful things he'd do when he finally had the time. He died just two months after taking his pension. The cause of death was cigarette smoking, and once again a habit had messed up the most careful planning.

YOU can blow your mind on just one bad narcotic trip. You can drink yourself to death in one evening. And you can develop a lifetime smoking habit in just a few days. How about it? Is there a place in your future for a costly habit that you might not be able to break? Think about it. Plan. And make the sensible decision. Stay away from the negative elements that can ruin your future.

CHAPTER 28

RECORDERS

DO you own a cassette tape recorder? Do you own two? Three?

IF you said "no" to one, then you have revealed a great deal about yourself. "No" to two tells a bit more, and if you said "yes" to three, then chances are you have discovered something about tape recorders that I've discovered. Tape recorders are the greatest breakthrough in the field of education in the past century. Let me repeat that. Tape recorders are the greatest breakthrough in the field of education in the past century. Tape recorders changed my luck. They have changed my life.

OH, I'm sure that you believe I'm guilty of overstatement IF you haven't learned for yourself just what a cassette tape recorder can do for you.

AN inexpensive tape recorder can put you in close personal contact with some of the greatest minds in the world. And this can be done during periods of the day that you are now wasting.

HOW many minutes a day do you spend in your automobile? If you are a commuter, how many minutes do you spend waiting for a train or a bus or traveling on that train or bus? What do you do with this time?

HARDLY a day passes in my life that I don't spend at least an hour in my automobile. My home is just a few minutes away from my office and yet I make at least two round trips a day. I used to waste this time. Our city is a bit unique in that it is bisected by two railroads. Busy railroads. And the chances that you will be tied up at a railroad crossing are something that would make Oddsmaker Jimmy The Greek's mouth water. And would you believe it, most people complain bitterly about these delays. Since I had a cassette tape recorder installed in my car the delays don't bother me. I rather welcome them. The reason is that I spend those waiting moments listening to great ideas. I have converted my automobile into a traveling classroom.

Just recently a company I work with checked out the cost of installing AM-FM Stereo Radio-cassette units in their new com-

pany cars locally, as opposed to having standard radios installed in their cars by the car dealer, and they found they could buy the combination units and have them installed cheaper than the auto manufacturer's installed AM unit. In other words, they were converting to a much better unit at a savings.

OUR local library now has a rather extensive Cassette Tape Lending Program. Recently, when visiting Minneapolis, I dropped in at their main library and discovered that nearly every section of the library not only had books but they also carried records and tapes on all subjects. Many books have been edited and presented audibly on cassette tapes. Today it is possible to drive your automobile and absorb all of the information contained in a book.

YOU can take a foreign language and become quite proficient in speaking that language in your spare moments. Doctors keep up-to-date daily in this manner. In my own personal case, most of the exciting ideas I have absorbed have come to me by means of cassette tapes.

OH, listening to tapes is one thing you can do with a cassette recorder but maybe you have something difficult that you must learn? Read it aloud into your own recorder and then listen to it a dozen times. Loop tapes are available that go around and around repeating the same message. One professional speaker I work with puts three minute humor monologues on tape and listens to them again and again until they are truly his.

IF you really seek to communicate, it is a good idea to listen to what you are saying. If you have a speech to give, then give it aloud and record it. Then listen to it as an outsider. What is this person saying, and how well is the point being made? Do the same thing with your correspondence. Read that letter aloud and see how well it sounds.

IF you give a speech, record it. Listen to what you said and see how many ways you could improve your performance.

WHEN you attend a meeting and they have a featured speaker, tape the talk. So many people believe incorrectly that once is enough. An idea or a concept is not really yours until you encounter that idea five or six times. When you buy a self improvement cassette program, listen to it again and again. The words on the tape do not change, but you do as your understanding grows. As you grow, the message takes on new meaning.

My dear friend Cavett Robert often quotes a set of statistics that indicate that the average salesperson spends two years of his life in the bathroom. Not at once, mind you, but that is the accumulated time spent. He spends three years of his life at the dining table having meals. And the average American salesperson spends the accumulated total of five years of his life in his automobile. I've seen reports of research in both Los Angeles and Detroit that if the average driving commuter would listen to educational tapes to and from work, he could absorb the equivelent of a batchelors degree in knowledge in just six years. Does a cassette recorder make sense to you now?

When you listen to a recorded message again and again you encounter a technique called "spaced repetition". When we read a book, if you are like me, you understand about 25% of what you read. You might retain only 10% of that. By listening to a tape again and again you go through what I call layers of learning. Let's say that the first time you listen to a tape you find it entertaining, stimulating and yes. . .even educational. If the tape is by a professional speaker then chances are he had ideas whizzing by you at a rapid rate. You were being exposed to all sorts of exciting concepts, quotes from the past and thoughts that were foreign to you. Let's say that you really absorbed 25% of what you heard. Now you go through that tape again, only this time you have a foundation of understanding on which to build. You already know what is coming, only this time you seem to take one step further along the road to understanding. If you listen to that tape once a day for a week you will discover that each time you learned something new. And you will also discover that the material is working its way into your subconscious mind and into your memory bank. You can recall some of the material. Every time you listen to a tape, you understand a bit more of it. Now, if you simply go back to that tape once a month the material will stay fresh in your mind.

For several years now I have had a creative writing course available on cassette tapes. There are a number of writers who have listened to my tapes and become successful writers. I have checked back with the most successful and find that the ones who really soar have listened to my tapes as many as twenty times each. One writer who now has three successful books on the market wrote me that she listened to my tapes as she did the ironing for her large family. She listened to each tape at least twenty times before going on to the next. She wrote that the tapes gave her the confidence she needed to carry on.

Recently she wrote me that she goes back to the tapes every six months for a refresher course.

I hesitated buying my first tape recorder for nearly a year and when I finally bought it, it paid for itself within three hours. I remember that I had a writing assignment for a magazine called Archery World and was headed for an International Tournament in Detroit. I bought the tape recorder on an impulse and the minute I walked into Cobo Hall I found a large crowd gathered around one archer. He had just three more shots to go for a perfect score. The first perfect score ever shot in International Competition. I reached for my camera and started shooting. Three. Two. And then with that final arrow the crowd roared and I simply reached for my new tape recorder. I walked up to that stunned, happy man and said, "I'm Art Fettig, with Archery World and I want to know what it feels like to shoot the first perfect score in International Competition." He told me. That one interview more than paid for my tape recorder, but that day I went on to interview half a dozen of the world's finest archers and I sold every interview.

Now I use tape recorders in many ways. I tape every speech I give and listen to it to find out how I'm doing. When I want to learn new speech material I record it and then listen to it again and again. I have tapes going in my car whenever I'm on the road. I do some dictation for a secretary on my tape recorder. I've taped my own end of telephone conversations with prospects just to hear what I'm saying. I use a tape recorder in my car to capture ideas that I have while traveling along the expressway. When I am doing research in the library I avoid making long notes by simply reading book passages into my recorder. When I do an interview with a celebrity I use my recorder. It is easy to tape a question and answer session and avoids the embarrassment of misquoting.

There is no need to spend an arm and a leg for a cassette recorder. There are a number of good machines available for under $30. If you don't want to go to the expense of having one installed in your car you can purchase a cigar lighter adapter so you won't be burning up batteries while listening in your auto.

Now I want to tell you about my friend Max Stark. Every time I think about cassette tapes I think about Max. Max was born in Germany and he was a pastry man. He studied the pastry business not only in Germany but he worked in France, Switzerland, Italy and Austria learning to make the most delicious pastry possible. Then in 1952 Max moved his family to Chicago and within six years he had worked his way up to Vice President of one of the largest retail bakeries in America. As Max looked around him in Chicago he felt that there must be some better place to raise his family and so after quite a search he discovered Battle Creek, Michigan. Max took a job in a bakery as a pastry man and he worked in the early morning hours of the day preparing wedding cakes and specials but at that time there wasn't a great demand for Max's Dobish or Prince Regenten Torts. Battle Creek wasn't ready just then for the most fantastic Napoleon Slices or Florentiners that Max could produce with such care and joy. And so Max found himself with burning energy and too little work to occupy his time. He made a brief investigation into the field of life insurance but it didn't seem like the right field for Max. Then one day Max called me on the phone and asked that I drop over to his house. When I arrived he produced a tray full of Black Forest Torts. These are indescribable creations made from cherries that are soaked in Cherry Brandy for four days. Well, I tried two and then Max got to the point. "Art," he began, "I'm going into the Real Estate business and I want to know what you can do to make me successful."

That sounded like an easy order. After all, Max was one of the most hardworking, determined men I have ever met. "Max," I said, "I want you to buy a cassette recorder. It doesn't have to be an expensive one. You will just be listening to talking tapes . . .no music. I'm going to give you two sets of tapes. I want you to spend fifteen minutes every day of your life listening to these tapes. I want you to listen to the first one five times and then to the second one five times and so on. . .every day you spend fifteen minutes."

If my memory is correct I gave Max the Cavett Robert set of tapes on Human Engineering and the Earl Nightengale tapes titled "Lead The Field."

After that when I saw Max he was busy running from one prospect to another. He worked every day and he was doing strange things. Max was knocking on people's doors and saying, "I've got somebody who is interested in buying a home in this neighborhood. Would you be interested in selling?"

Crazy things like. . .well. . .to do this one Max had to go out of town. Max bought up a batch of stringers. . .flags. . .and he had to have a painter make up a set of signs saying something that no signs had said in our Battle Creek area for a long, long time. It was old stuff. Not really "in." Those signs said, "Open House" and on Sundays when other realtors were home complaining about how slow business was in the area, Max was out showing a house to all comers.

In his first year in the Real Estate business Max Stark sold One million, two hundred and fifty thousand dollars worth of real estate. The second year he sold two million. One day I cornered him and I said to him, "Max, what is your secret? What is the one key to your great continued success in the Real Estate business?" Max laughed and he said, "It is those lousy tapes you gave me, Art. Every day for fifteen minutes I listen to those tapes. Again and again and again. . .why I know the material in those tapes better than the men who made the tapes. There is something strange about those tapes though. . .every time I listen to the tapes I learn something. Oh, the tapes don't change. They are the same tapes that you gave me to begin with. Of course I have added to my collection, but when I listen to those tapes again and again I found that while the tapes haven't changed, I have. My base of experience keeps growing and those dynamic ideas and their potential grow as I grow."

When Max first told me he had sold two million in his second year I kidded him. "Max, how could you, why there isn't two million dollars worth of Real Estate in Battle Creek." He just grinned and replied, "Well, Art, sometimes you have to turn it over a couple of times."

It was during Max's second year in the real estate business that he made one of those breakthrough discoveries that change people's lives and put them ahead of the whole pack. One day Max made the unbelievable discovery that most people never make. Here it is. . .the one idea that spelled greatness for Max in the Real Estate Business. It is an idea that could be applied to many businesses. Here it is. . .kids coming out of high school don't have enough money to buy One Hundred Thousand Dollar houses. Let me repeat that. Kids coming out of high school don't have enough money to buy One Hundred Thousand Dollar Houses. It was shortly after that, that Max made his second greatest discovery. Kids coming out of college can't afford One Hundred Thousand Dollar houses.

Now that might not sound like much of a breakthrough in thinking to you, but Max carried that thinking a little farther. He said to himself, "Maximillion, (You see, Max was a million dollar thinker even then.) He said, Maximillion, if they can't afford One Hundred Thousand Dollar Houses, what can they afford?" And the answer was apartments. And Max began to buy apartments. First he bought nicer apartments. He took his clients, and he said to them, "I am your Realtor for life."

When you rent from Max you must take a one year lease. The only way you can get out of that lease is to rent something nicer. And if you buy a home from Max then he tears up the lease.

Max knows the birthdays of all of his tenants. They get birthday cards from Max. If your name appears in the newspaper and it is good news Max sends you the clipping with congratulations. If you have a birth in the family Max calls and asks if you need a bigger place. When you get a promotion Max is willing to help you celebrate your good fortune with a larger home. Max cares. Max is there with you all the way and most of Max's clients stick with him because he really has their interests in mind.

I called Max last night just to bring myself up to date. Max owns a motel now. And the biggest home on the nicest lake in this area. Max just bought a 200 horsepower boat and do you know what he wanted to talk about? About Tarts. A bakery has just opened up right next to Max's Real Estate office and he has taken that bakery on as a personal challenge. He slips in there at 4'o'clock in the morning and works with their bakers showing them all of the secrets that he spent so many years learning. And he is as happy as the owner that crowds are now lining up every day just to buy that fabulous pastry that only a master like Max could produce. He told me to be sure and try the Hazel Nut and Mocca Torts. "Those I do myself," he said proudly.

So the lucky idea that I found from Max Stark is one of excellence. Max listens to cassette tapes better than anyone I ever met. He listens every morning and then he goes out and puts those ideas into action. For lucky ideas have no magic at all unless they are applied.

I am so sold on the value of the cassette tape as an educational device that I sometimes reveal to an audience something that I'm not all that proud of. That is the fact that I completed my formal education at age eighteen when I graduated from the University of Detroit High School. I've taken a few night classes but I do not have a single college credit to my name. I have personal clients, five of them, with Doctor's degrees and they hire me to write their speech material. I have clients that I write for who are now Chairmen of the Boards of some major corporations. I am often asked to lecture at Universities and quite often it is to teacher groups. I have addressed management groups from many of our major industries. I hope you'll take this puffery in the proper light. What I am trying to say is that people have respect for my ability to convey ideas and for the ideas that I share with them. Nearly all of the education that I have managed to absorb has come through the medium of cassette tapes. I try to find time to read but I really do very little reading. I seek out three or four stimulating seminars each year, but at nearly every seminar I attend, I obtain cassette tapes of the material so that I can really absorb it later in my automobile.

If you do not have a cassette tape player in your auto, in your home, in your place of business. If you are missing the stimulation, the encouragement, the wealth of knowledge that is available through this medium then this one idea can bring a whole new dimension to your life.

Cassette tapes have changed my whole life. Just try them and you too will discover their power.

If you would like me to help you select the tapes that I believe will help you the most just send me a note telling me about your goals, your background and your special interests and I will try to recommend tapes that will help you achieve your goals. If you work for a company that is interested in training its employees in their automobiles just include that information and I will make an effort to recommend materials for a company sponsored tape library that will serve the needs of all employees. Just write me. . .Art Fettig, at 31 East Ave. S., Battle Creek, Michigan, 49017.

CHAPTER 29

"EFFORT"

OVER at Columbia University there was a coach named Lou Little, and Lou Little wasn't famous for winning games. Lou Little was famous for taking boys and turning them into men. He had a special talent for causing growth. And one year a kid named John showed up for the Varsity Football tryouts. He wasn't a big kid. Not the greatest coordination. . .but inside, John had something special. . .something called "spirit," and when they got to cutting down the team, John wasn't cut. Sophomore year John made the Varsity and he was there on time for every practice. . .never missed, and John suited up for every game, but that first year John never got into a game. The next year it was the same thing. Never missed a practice, suited up for every game and never played. But Lou Little kept John on the team because John had something special. He was the inner cheerleader on that team. Got the guys up for the game, kept the enthusiasm high. . .and then in his Senior year. . .it was near the close of the season, and once again John remained on the bench. Funny thing though, John never asked to play. He knew what his role was. It was his job to keep the spirit up and he did it well. Well, one afternoon Lou Little got a telephone call from John's mother, and she said, "Lou, I know how John respects you and that's why I'm calling you. You see my husband, John's father, just had a coronory attack and died and I want you to tell John to come right home and help me with the funeral and everything, because you see, with his father gone, John is all I have left." And so Lou Little called John in and explained it, and he said, "John, it is near the end of the season and with your dad gone it is more important than ever that you get good grades and graduate. And so when you get back, if you don't want to come back with the team we'll understand."

TWO weeks later John showed up on the practice field all suited up, and he went right up to Lou Little and he said, "Coach, I want to start that game on Saturday." And Lou thought about it. . .what the heck, here this kid had been with the team three years, never missed a practice. . .never missed a game and he'd never let him play. He figured the least he could do was to let him in on the opening play. . .and well. . .if the kid screwed up he could always pull him out.

JOHN started that game, and you know. . .Lou Little never pulled him out. That kid played the greatest sixty minutes of football they ever saw at Columbia. He was in on every play. Ran like a Crazy Legs. Passed like a. . .Tarkenton. . .blocked every play. . .and when the game was over the other team couldn't figure out what happened because they were picked to win by two touchdowns and they lost by two. And John's own teammates couldn't understand what had happened. . .but the most confused man of all was Lou Little. He went into the

locker room and he finally found John on the rub down table and he said, "John, I'm supposed to be a professional judge of men and talents. I just can't understand what happened on that field today. In all that time that you were on the team I never saw anything to indicate that you could play great football like that. I'm totally confused. Maybe you can help me out and explain this to me, John."

AND John looked down for a minute and then he looked up and he smiled and said. "First of all coach, I want to apologize to you for asking to play like that. . .but you see, I just had to play that game today. This is the only chance my dad would have to see me play."

AND Lou looked confused and he said, "Now wait a minute John, I don't get it. You buried your father just two weeks ago."

JOHN got a serious look on his face and slowly he said, "I know that coach. . .but you see all my life my father was blind, and he never saw me do anything. I figured this was the only chance he'd have to see me play."

JOHN believed that. He gave the game all he had and something wonderful happened that day. One hundred ten percent effort. I think that is the secret behind every lucky athlete.

THE Lou Little story is a sort of classic on the lecture platform. I first heard it on a tape and I was very moved. . .yet the way it was told made me go to work and rewrite the whole thing. I've told the story many, many times and it never fails to bring a tear to my eye.

I'VE written to Columbia University, trying to verify the story and I've received no reply. Just last week I had a visit with a great platform professional by the name of Bill Gove, and we talked about that story. "That isn't the Lou Little story, Art. . . you've got it messed up." "It was the Herman Hickman story." Another seasoned platform veteran joined us, and he too knew the story. . .a slightly different version of it. . .and with this version it wasn't Columbia University. It wasn't Lou Little. The kids name wasn't John. Stories change. . .they get better and worse with the retelling, but there is one thing I know about this story. It is a powerful tale. It moves audiences to tears, and more than that, it inspires greater effort. Should I abandon the story, a story of such beauty? No, possibly it can provide a bit of insight into this business of lecturing that we engage in. A speech is made up of many, many ingredients. In a way it is a theatrical performance. A careful, well planned mixing of tested ingredients. Entertaining, yes. Inspiring. . .hopefully. And in my book there is something else to aim for as a goal. I want my audiences to have a good time, but more than that. . .I want them to go home with a determination to get a full measure of joy from living. . .and that comes only from greater involvement.

CHAPTER 30

PUT IT IN WRITING

There is an old story going around about a young man who wasn't too eager to go into the service and so when they gave him his physical he found himself in front of the Army psychiatrist. He rushed up to the doctor and said, "Doc, you got to OK me. I want to get in there and fight. Just give me a rifle doc and I'll shoot 'em. . .I'll shoot them all. And when I run out of bullets, Doc, I'll use that bayonette. And if they take that away from me I'll hit 'em with my fist. . .I'll hit 'em doc and I will kill them with my bare hands. . .you got to OK me Doc and let me at them." The doctor looks at the young man and says, "You're crazy." And the young man says. . ."Write it down, Doc, Write it down."

SO you plan to Dare. You plan to D A R E something different. Something exciting. You plan to become lucky and successful in some endeavor and you feel like a W I L D T U R K E Y about to jump barefoot into the excitement of living.

GREAT. BRAVO. CHEERS. But a word of advice. Put it in writing. Put your plan, your goal, your idea in writing and see how it suddenly catches fire. See how it gains momentum by the simple process of writing it down.

I'VE interviewed a number of outstanding successes recently and every one of them admitted that at the critical turning point in his life each one of them had taken a pen in hand and written a series of goals he hoped to reach.

BANDLEADER, Stan Kenton, Master of Artistry in Rhythm, recently told me, "Things happened much faster than I thought they would. I had certain goals that I had picked but the goals seemed to pass so quickly that I felt kind of confused at times for lack of direction because I thought it would take longer to attain certain things than it did."

MR. Perfect. Les "Jugger" Gervais, one of the nation's finest professional archers, told me, "You have to set your goals higher all the time. Just a little bit higher, not too high. Where you know it's not impossible to reach. Then you can usually come pretty close to it." Jugger shot a perfect 300 score at Las Vegas recently. He believes that writing it down makes it come true. He writes down notes on his style and form in an effort for constant improvement.

SOMEHOW writing it down feeds the data into your subconscious mind a little clearer, and when you let your mind know exactly where you want to go, then you simply get there a lot quicker.

WRITING it down brings it into focus. Clarifies it. Makes you pin down exactly what you wish to achieve. This simple act eliminates a lot of spinning of the wheels.

TRY it, Pick a goal. Set a target date. Now get to work making it come true. But one more thing. B E L I E V E. That's right. BELIEVE that it will come true. Start acting as if you are certain you will achieve your goal. Read that goal every morning when you get up and every night before you go to sleep. Read it, believe it, and start doing the things you feel you should do to make it come true.

THIS simple formula of writing it down and believing works. It works for the young and old, male and female. Once you get moving, your momentum will carry you over many of the obstacles that might have previously stopped you.

TALK to someone you know who is a real success. Ask him or her about goals. About writing it down. You'll be amazed to learn that most people who are successful found success by setting their goals clearly, firmly, and then pitching in to reach those goals.

I dare you to write it down. Goal writing produces luck.

CHAPTER 31

PLAY ON THE TEAM THAT WILL HAVE YOU

The next lucky idea came to me from my son, Daniel.

Whoever said that we learn more from our children than they could ever learn from us made a wise observation.

I'm sure you have heard the old maxim, "Play the hand that's dealt you." Well, with Daniel I learned that same idea, only it would have to be rewritten to read, "Play on the team that will have you."

Daniel has had an interest in basketball since he was just twelve years old. In my first book, "*It Only Hurts When I Frown*" I told about the frustration that a parent feels when his son is ignored by the coach and the game ends with your son still sitting on the bench. Since that book hit the market I guess a thousand people have come to me and told me how they had shared that same feeling.

Daniel made the Junior Varsity team at St. Philip when he was a Sophomore. The team was loaded with talent and Daniel spent a great deal of the time on the bench that season. Then the next year he went out for Varsity but he didn't make the team. He tried to get on the Junior Varsity but they were building a young team and well. . .Daniel couldn't make Junior Varsity either. It was quite a blow to him but instead of moping around the house Daniel went out and found a team at one of the local gyms. He was gone a lot of the time and he'd come home all tired out but happy that he was playing basketball.

One day I asked him about his team and the fellows on the team and it was then that Daniel told me, "Dad, those other guys really play for keeps. And you know, I'm the only white kid on the team."

That about floored me. I pride myself on my racial tolerance but this was a bit much for me. I tried to use tact when I said, "That's fine that you are playing, Dan, but wasn't there a white team that you could get on?" He said, "Yeah Dad, I guess there was, but you see, this team of blacks really hustles. You look around you, Dad, at the pro's. An awful lot of them are black.

They really know how to play this game, and I want to learn all I can."

Well, they won some and lost some and Dan gave it all he had that season. Then at the end of the season they went to Grand Rapids for some sort of hair-brained tournaments. They had to get there early in the morning and there was a series of elimination games. If you won then you had to play another team. And if you won again then you had to play another. And as the day wore on Dan's team played one game after the other. They started at 7AM and it was after 8PM when they finished and their team had won everything. They had the championship and they had the title and they had this big golden trophy. It was while they were driving home from the tournament together in a crowded station wagon. . .all blacks but Daniel. . .and they got together and they voted who would get the trophy to keep . . .and well. . .they gave our Daniel that trophy.

Not that he ever did, but you'll never hear Daniel use the word "nigger." And nobody else had better when our Daniel is around.

Dan made the Varsity team at St. Philip the next year and oh, he wasn't the star of the team. He was in my eyes though. But when they had that sports banquet they passed out all of that praise for the team and all of those awards and it was the last thing on the program. The Father Owens Award for the kid that showed the most spirit. . .The most hustle. And I cried like only a Dad can when they called out Dan's name.

I guess the lesson is this. Play on the team that will have you and play your heart out. That's the only way to go through life . . .all out and finding the joy of effort all the way.

CHAPTER 32

"ASK"

IF you don't know, ask. That's right. IF YOU DON'T KNOW, ASK. Five little words that can change your whole life. Look at the thousands of novels that wouldn't have been if the central character had merely asked a simple, important question. Look at what is called TV entertainment. Nearly every story is based on one simple primary misunderstanding. A misunderstanding that would have been cleared up in a minute if someone had asked a simple question. Instead, the plot thickens and one misunderstanding is added to another until we have a complicated mess that is finally resolved when the fall guy gets around to asking his simple question and getting his simple answer.

LOOK at your life and it's problems. Aren't most problems the result of misunderstanding? A result of your not asking, or perhaps not answering clearly. Asking isn't a sign of ignorance, it's a sign of interest. While you are at this business of asking, make it a point to ask someone who knows. Do a little research.

HOW many times have you driven miles out of your way thru heavy traffic because you didn't take 30 seconds to pull into a gas station and ask? How many wrong buses have you boarded? How many wrong lines have you waited in?

THIS problem of asking is not a new one. There are proverbs in any language to cover this situation. The Danes have an old proverb that says, "He who is afraid of asking is ashamed of learning." The Italians say this, "Asking costs little." The Yiddish say it this way, "Better ask ten times than go astray once."

HENRY Ford once explained his ignorance of certain data an attacking lawyer was seeking by reminding the man that his success was not due to his brilliance but to the ability to know whom to ask when he needed an answer.

IF you have a medical problem, ask a doctor, and the sooner the better. If you have a legal question, get to a lawyer. Learn your way around the reference room of the local library; you'll be surprised at the number of successful people you run into there. Lucky people use resources readily available to all, but seldom used. Professional advice is one of the best investments you can make. The sooner you get good advice in any endeavor, the sooner you'll get started on the right road, on the right approach, on building the proper foundation for a successful venture. Think of your life as a building you are putting up brick by brick. A fellow who puts in a good foundation and then keeps adding bricks properly, ends up with a good result, but the guy who builds on quicksand ends up with a mess. You can avoid that quicksand by getting expert advice and you get that advice by asking.

DARING is great. All of the world's progress is a result of someone's dare, but while you are daring don't be afraid when something baffles you. Just Ask. And if you are still baffled, ask again and then again and again, and don't forget that old proverb, "Better ask ten times then go astray once."

CHAPTER 33

SELLING LUCKY

WE started out with a goal of collecting a good supply of Lucky Selling Ideas. Lucky ideas that could change your life. Put you in the top ten percent in your field.

IDEAS kept popping their heads onto my typewriter keyboard, shouting "Hear Me! Hear Me!"

AND yet, regretfully, not a single idea that we have presented in this book will change your luck for the better unless you do something about that idea. Ideas are useless without action.

CHANCE is what happens in your life. Luck is what you do about it. Luck is being prepared for good things to happen. Having the ability and the agility and the enthusiasm to make it happen.

SO often I've used the expression, "Good Luck!", and it was just a parting gesture. "Good Luck, Charlie!" Good Luck, Dorothy!" And what I really meant to say is that I wish you success, and happiness, and I wish you a life full of joy, and most of all I wish you love.

GOOD Luck to me is not winning a sweepstakes or lottery. It isn't finding the pot of gold at the base of the rainbow. Good Luck is living the good life, enjoying your work and your family and your God. And when people call me Mr. Lucky, I thank God for it.

SPARK
IDEAS

CHAPTER 34

GET UP DAD!

Our youngest son, David, is seventeen now. Six foot three and a half inches tall at least. It changes every week or so.

Six foot three and a half inches of growing boy and David is a fisherman. Everyone has a talent. That is my message to every audience I face and perhaps David's talent lies with the uncaught fish out there in this world.

If having a tough time in school is hereditary then David can blame me for rotten genes. As I watch him he reminds me of myself at his age. But sometimes David makes us so proud.

The other evening I was sitting in our den reading someone else's book and writing down some original thoughts for my speech when David kicked my foot and said, "Get up Dad."

David's foot is bigger than mine. David's foot just might be bigger than yours too. And when David gives you a kick you pay attention and David said "Get Up Dad!" and I looked up and there was David standing there in front of our television set with his hand on his heart.

You see, when our children were small they were just like the steps of a ladder in height. One, two, three, four. There was just about a year between them. Nancy, Daniel, Amy and David. And one day when they were about 9, 8, 7 and 6, they were all in the den with me and there was a football game about to go on. I looked at them and I said to myself, "We don't have many traditions in this family and I am a gonna start me one." So I stood up and put my hand over my heart and I said to the children, "Kids, that is the Star Spangled Banner they are playing and from now on in this house, whenever they play the Star Spangled Banner, let's all stand up and put our hands over our hearts and watch until it is over."

And somehow it stuck. And now when I'm reading in the den and David kicks me on the foot and says, "Get up Dad." Gee, it feels good.

CHAPTER 35

"PEOPLE"

ONE of the really nice things about traveling around the country giving speeches is the fact that you meet so many different kinds of people. And yet, people are pretty much the same no matter where I've traveled. People in Korea or Mexico. Japan, or yes, even Denver, Colorado. And I've met people in Texas and Minnesota, Chicago and Miami. . . . .and you know, people pretty well act the way you expect them to. If you expect them to treat you with courtesy and kindness and integrity, they usually come through for you. And if you expect them to shortchange you and treat you rudely, they usually fulfill your expectations. Because people react very quickly to the people they are dealing with.

ONE of the nice things I've discovered is that most of the people I come in contact with in my work are action people. Certainly you've heard it said many times that there are really three kinds of people. . .those who watch things happen. . . those who aren't even aware that anything is happening, and those who make things happen. Just a very small percentage of the people in this world make things happen, and yet, thank God, I get a great deal of exposure to those who make things happen. These are usually the happy people. The successful people. They have discovered their particular talents and they have devoted a part of their life to using their talents to making this a better world. People who make things happen usually work with other people. . .often young people. . .and they take others by the hand and help them to understand that they can be more productive, more successful. . .yes, much, much happier kinds of people.

IF I have discovered anything about people and about communicating with people, it is this. There is so much more to this business of communication than the mere use of words. You are what you are and the mere use of words cannot change that. What you are means much more to an audience than merely what you say. If you care about an audience they will sense this.

Selling, selling, selling. Ideas. Products. Services. Selling people on themselves and on you. That is what we hope we have helped you with. Selling yourself first and then your ideas, your hopes, your dreams.

There are those in this world who find the word "selling" repulsive. I would like to conclude with the answer to those who fail to grasp the importance of selling in this world. Perhaps my verse "Yes, We Are!" says it all.

We are salespeople. . .

We make this world hum a better tune.

We rise to the call "Complete!"

Adding that magic ingredient "Free"

To our Free Enterprise System.

We make choice possible,

And if somehow, you think,

Our product lacks the edge, we compensate.

You get more of us then. And that, my friend,

Is better than a silver handle.

We are salespeople. Thank God for it.

For we will keep you working.

Salespeople make this whole world hum.

We sell, we demonstrate and elecute

And use ten closes, unless you fail to buy.

And then we'll close ten times again,

And more if there be need,

Because the world demands our wares.

We wouldn't be just Doctors, Lawyers,

Presidents or Indian Chiefs.

We are SALESPEOPLE.

WHEN I walk on stage I have the feeling that I am a professional fighter.

I've trained. . . .I know about my opponent and I try very hard to land the first blow. I dance around. . .jab, weave, throw a hard left and a hard right. . .and after we get to know each other. . .after we have developed a mutual respect, then the fight scene turns into more of a sharing experience. We share good times and some information I feel is important, and then we have to say goodbye and move on to the next audience.

IF there is one key to communicating it must be the key of empathy. Unless you convince an audience that you understand their dreams and their needs then there is little hope for you and your message.

IF you can learn to communicate, there is no doubt that you will bite off a much greater chunk of life. You'll find a great deal more happiness, and success will come so fast that it will amaze you.

I hope in some small way that my book has helped you get it all together.

I WISH YOU— LOVE